A New Call to Mission

A New Call to Mission

Help for Perplexed Churches

Alan Neely

We are members now of that family of faith with ties deeper than any we have known before.

This brings us to the issue of continuing and deepening the belonging with Christ and His church, which constitutes the meaning of entrance and membership in the church. Too often the pilgrim on the Christian Way loses sight of the City whose builder and maker is God, and settles down in flat country—a displaced person with no worldly home and no kingdom destiny, the sad-face refugee of a battle that was to have taken a world for Christ. The cross may be mentioned, but our hearts do not stir. The symbol is dead: the symbol which had the power to interpret our life together, to hold it, to extend it, and to give it new dimensions. We can even hold in our hands broken bread, and we can put to our lips poured-out wine, and nothing burns within our souls. The urgency is lost, the belonging is lost because we were not aware that they could be lost.

The reasons for this may be many, but often it is because we have forgotten that one of our primary responsibilities is the nurturing of our own members.

—Elizabeth O'Connor, *Call to Commitment* (1963).

Smyth & Helwys Publishing, Inc.
6316 Peake Road
Macon, Georgia 31210-3960
1-800-747-3016

Printed in the United States of America.

Alan Neely

The paper used in this publication meets the minimum requirements of American National Standard for Information Sciences—Permanence of Paper for Printed Library Materials.
ANSI Z39.48–1984. (alk. paper)

Library of Congress Cataloging-in-Publication Data

Neely, Alan
A new call to mission: Help for perplexed churches.
ISBN
pp. cm.
1. Missions--Theory. 2. Missions--Global. 3. Missions--North America. 4. Mission history. 5. Local congregation and mission. 6. World Religion. 7. Christian mission in 20th and 21st centuries. 8. International Mission Board, SBC. 9. The Cooperative Baptist Fellowship, SBC. 10. The Alliance of Baptists.
Permissions for quotations (prior to each chapter) have been granted.

CIP

ISBN 1-57312-296-3

Contents

FOREWORD

Ever since meeting Alan Neely, I have been blessed by his friendship, stimulated by his scholarship, encouraged by his faithfulness, and challenged by his witness. He is a gift to the Baptist family and a respected missiologist beyond his own faith tradition. *A New Call to Mission* is a fresh and relevant tool for churches seeking to be on mission in a troubled world. This is an outstanding workbook. It informs and it inspires. It disturbs and it encourages. It is a resource and a reference that can be used again and again.

A New Call to Mission is going to do just what its subtitle promises: it will help perplexed churches. It will help them by giving a biblical model for mission, a succinct analysis for the context of mission, a historical survey of mission and a pointed, sometimes painful, description of three channels for cooperative mission in Baptist life. But perhaps what is most significant about this volume is the practical steps it suggests for churches to rediscover a passion for mission.

Jesus established only one mission organization, the Church. Conventions, Fellowships and Alliances surely have their place and can be helpful, but only to the degree that they serve the Church. And when the Church, in its functioning congregational and cooperative life, awakens to the glorious privilege of incarnating Christ in the world and becoming a part of God's mission, it will be a great day.

One of the exciting developments as we enter the 21st century is the recovery and reemergence of the priority of global missions in the local church. Churches are rediscovering that they "exist by mission as a fire exists by burning." Yet they are also rediscovering that they need help in discerning and deciding as to how they will engage in mission.

My sincere prayer is that God will use this volume to awaken the conscience of Baptists, renew the spirit of Baptists and contribute greatly to a fresh impetus for world mission.

Daniel Vestal
Atlanta, Georgia
Coordinator, Cooperative Baptist Fellowship
March 1999

PREFACE

In 1996 I presented a research paper on the history and work of the Southern Baptist Foreign Mission Board to an ecumenical group of missiologists who met at Stony Point, New York. Mine was one of four studies of various mission boards and agencies in the United States. Discussion of the papers occupied the entire weekend. A year later a pastor in Baltimore, Maryland asked me to help his church leaders understand and evaluate the mission program of the Southern Baptist Foreign Mission Board and compare it with the mission endeavors of the Cooperative Baptist Fellowship and of the Alliance of Baptists. Like many other pastors and church leaders, they were quite aware that radical changes had occurred in the SBC since 1979. They sensed that these changes were affecting the mission work, but were less knowledgeable in regard to the specific differences. I agreed to do the project. At the time I had only the study of the Foreign Mission Board. As I began in-depth analysis of the mission program of the Cooperative Baptist Fellowship and the Alliance of Baptists, I discovered how formidable the task would be.

Analyzing and evaluating the work of the SBC's Foreign Mission Board (now the International Mission Board), the Cooperative Baptist Fellowship, and the Alliance of Baptists is somewhat like trying to compare a canoe, a 100-foot yacht, and the *Queen Elizabeth 2*. All of them float, each moving in a discernible direction. If you board any one of them, it will deliver you to a specified destination. However, they are not equal in size, speed, passenger capacity, or crew requirement.

When I began and ended this study, my desire was to be objective and not to elevate one agency at the expense of the others. Each has its own positive qualities and all are doing good things. None, however, is without its deficiencies, and those who support one or more of these programs would do well to reflect on what their critics are saying.

The evaluations of the three mission efforts—that of the IMB, the CBF, and the Alliance—represent honest and, I believe, objective appraisals. They reflect the perceptions and judgments of many pastors, teachers, laypersons, missionaries, trustees, and mission administrators—people vitally interested in and committed to the mission of the Church in the world. Over the past three years I have interviewed scores of these people, including knowledgeable persons working for each of the three agencies. I have asked them and other colleagues and friends to read and critique portions or all of the manuscript. The feedback they provided and their insights and suggestions have been exceedingly helpful. Many will recognize their comments and ideas reflected in the text. I am not suggesting, however, that oversights, misstatements, or inaccuracies can be blamed on them or anyone else. I must assume responsibility for what I have written.

I would like to acknowledge every individual who has given an interview, participated in discussion groups, or has read parts or all of the manuscript. Some who work for these agencies—especially for the International Mission Board—prefer not to be identified. I do, however, express gratitude to John Ewing Roberts, pastor of Woodbrook Baptist Church in Baltimore, who first invited me to appraise the three mission programs for his church leaders. Also, without the encouragement of Howard Roberts, now pastor of the Ravensworth Baptist Church in Annandale, Virginia, and Robert Albritton, pastor of the Millbrook Baptist Church in Raleigh, North Carolina, this effort would have gathered dust. Both allowed me occasions to test material with groups in their congregations. Without the input of these people, I doubtless would have made more blunders than are now apparent.

Among those who have read parts of the work are Thomas Bland and his wife Eunice Smith Bland, Anne Neil, Mary Strauss, Stan Hastey, and Jeanette Holt. Dr. John LeMond, friend and professor of Church History at the Lutheran Theological Seminary in Hong Kong, read and provided valuable counsel in relation to the discussion of China. My wife Virginia, always supportive but nonetheless critical, has read and re-read all that is here. I am in their debt.

Many other friends and colleagues have contributed to my thinking about the Church and mission, and they deserve to be mentioned. To attempt this would be futile. One person, however, merits special acknowledgment—Ms. Kim Mick—for she has provided invaluable technological assistance.

Alan Neely
Raleigh, North Carolina
January 1999

Part 1

In previous times "people in the church at home knew very little about the world 'out there.'... Today, travel, international business and education have altered drastically the way people feel about the world mission field."

—Paul McKaughan, Delanna and William O'Brien
Choosing a Future for U.S. Missions (1998).

Chapter 1

The New Context for Mission

Generally Christians know that the contemporary world is significantly different from the world of the nineteenth and early twentieth centuries. Yet many continue to wonder why today we do mission work differently than in previous generations. The single explanation is that we are living in a new political, social, economic, and religious context.

What Happened to the Way We Used to Do Missions?

Since the mid-1940s humankind has experienced a series of changes so radical that no one anticipated them and few are more than marginally aware of them. Little appears fixed or stable. These revolutionary changes began during World War II, and they increased in number and intensity thereafter.

The Cold War and the Aftermath

Even before the Allied victory was certain and the peace treaties signed, it was evident that the world would soon become locked in a new struggle—a conflict of immense proportions that came to be known as the Cold War. This prolonged political and economic strife between East and West was fueled by mutual suspicion, fear, and animosity. It divided the world with the Soviet Union and its allies on one side and the United States and its NATO (North Atlantic Treaty Organization) allies on the other. The Cold War continued for more than four decades, moderated only partially by the non-aligned nations who in the mid-1950s began referring to themselves as "the Third World."[1] The Third World, however, simply became a new ideological and military battleground for the two super powers.

The End of Colonialism

Meanwhile, most of the Asian and African colonies that had been dominated for generations either by Great Britain, the Netherlands, France, Germany, Italy, Portugal, or the United States gained their political independence. New conflicts erupted in most of these new nations as well as in other parts of the world, particularly in Latin America. The impact of these developments on Christian missions and missionaries became evident quickly.

Those areas of the world dominated by the communists, such as China, the Soviet Union, and Cuba, were closed to missionaries. Some non-communist nations, such as Burma, expelled missionaries. Other governments, such as in India and Malaysia, made it increasingly difficult for foreign missionaries to enter or to remain for extended periods of time. Even in the nations where missionaries had worked for decades and could continue to do so, leaders of the national churches moved deliberately to end missionary control. As early as 1947 it was clear that in the post-war world the role of the foreign missionary—if there were to be a role—would be different. In country after country Christian schools and hospitals were either nationalized, that is, taken over by the government, or they came under the control of national synods, presbyteries, conferences, and conventions. These synods, presbyteries, conferences, and conventions were led by nationals who demanded a say in the number and types of missionaries they would welcome into their countries.

Islamic Countries

Several but not all the Islamic nations were closed to missionaries. Others permitted the entry of missionary doctors, nurses, and teachers, but prohibited them from engaging in direct evangelization. Other predominantly Muslim lands, however, continued to be open to missionaries—Indonesia, Bangladesh, Pakistan, Iran, and Egypt, for example. Yet, with few exceptions, religious freedom in these Muslim lands has not resulted in large numbers of converts to the Christian faith. Evangelization is exceedingly difficult in Islamic cultures, primarily because becoming a Christian is not considered an individual spiritual decision. It is considered a repudiation of one's family and culture. In some Muslim lands Christian conversion and baptism are deemed political acts of treason to one's people and nation.

Israel, a Special Case

In Israel all are guaranteed by law the freedom to *practice* their faith, but they are not guaranteed the right or freedom to *change* their faith. Missionaries were living and working in Palestine and throughout the Ottoman Empire long before Israel was created by the United Nations in 1948, and missionaries are permitted to live and work in Israel today, though generally they do not refer to themselves as "missionaries." "Fraternal workers" and "religious representatives" are more common designations. As far as evangelization is concerned, missionaries in Israel have far more success with the Palestinian or Arab population, twenty percent of which is Christian, than with the Jews. Also, from time to time laws passed by the Israeli government threaten penalties for any Jew who would convert to Christianity or Islam as well as for anyone who tries to "entice" a Jew to convert. Israel, therefore, remains a religiously and politically divided land—Jewish, Christian, Muslim—but it is decidedly tilted in favor of Judaism despite the fact that most Jews living in Israel are secular.[2]

What about the "New Mission Fields" of China and Eastern Europe?

With the opening of China to western diplomacy and trade in the 1960s and the collapse of the Soviet Union in the late 1980s, a new world began to take shape. We are only beginning to learn how to live in a post-Cold War world with its new challenges, new threats, and new opportunities.

Some Christians in the west regard China and Eastern Europe as newly opened mission fields, needy and "ready for harvest." To what extent is this perception accurate?

China

Legally it is not possible to gain entry into China as a missionary. Yet since the late 1970s thousands of Christians have been permitted to enter and engage in commercial, industrial, and educational endeavors. Some well-meaning Christian enthusiasts, however, do not accept these concessions. They enter China posing as teachers, technologists, or business people when their true motive for being there is to evangelize. This is not only illegal, but risky and probably shortsighted.

The Chinese government welcomes business people, technicians, and teachers from the outside, and does not require foreign Christians living and working in China to deny or conceal their faith. Neither do they force these Christians to remain silent when a Chinese citizen asks religious questions or wants to discuss matters of faith. However, they do not permit traditional evangelization of the Chinese people or the introduction of western religious sectarianism. The Protestant churches associated with the China Christian Council (CCC) refer to themselves as "post-denominational," not Baptist, Methodist, or Presbyterian.[3] Likewise, the Roman Catholic Church there functions independently from Rome. Since the churches were allowed to re-open in 1979 at least 12,000 congregations now function as Protestant churches with their own buildings. Additional thousands worship in house churches.[4] The government and many of the Chinese Christian leaders, however, are determined to prevent the re-introduction of Protestant denominationalism or the control of the Catholic Church in China by the Vatican. Rightly or wrongly, sectarianism and the domination of the Chinese churches by foreigners are associated with the colonial and missionary era in China's history.

Foreign Christians traveling or residing in China are free to attend worship in any church. There are, however, no Christian schools in China except for seminaries. The law forbids the establishment of a religious primary or secondary school. Schools organized by minority people such as the Muslim Uigurs are allowed. The Uigurs choose to teach their children religious lessons even though doing so is strictly forbidden among the Han majority. It is possible to teach English or computer science or any number of subjects at the university level, but those arrangements at this level have nothing to do with the China Christian Council. The CCC strictly relates to ecclesiastical matters. The Amity Foundation, a social service organization related to the CCC, does place teachers in teachers' colleges throughout China, but there are hundreds of other teachers in China who either make their own arrangements or enter China through one of the organizations that places teachers in China. Being associated with and working under the CCC, however, is currently a divisive issue among certain Protestant missionary–sending bodies. Most of the historic Protestant mission agencies readily cooperate with the CCC, but some evangelical denominations and para-church groups are unwilling to limit their activities to educational and technical assistance. Also, some believe the CCC is connected too closely to the communist government. These evangelicals are so convinced that the Chinese are not hearing the gospel and that the CCC is an impediment that they intentionally ignore the legal restrictions and send "missionaries" to evangelize the Chinese while pretending to be in China for other reasons.

Eastern Europe

For the most part, restrictions placed on foreigners traveling and residing in Eastern Europe are considerably less than those imposed by China. For this reason, many more Christians from North America, Western Europe, and Asia—especially from Korea—are going to Romania, Lithuania, Russia, the Ukraine, Belarus, and Azerbaijan, and other republics that formerly constituted the Soviet Union. Though evangelizing is permitted in these countries, much of the mission activity in Eastern Europe raises profound questions for ecumenically and culturally sensitive Christians.

Assume, for example, that someone in your congregation proposes a "mission trip" to Lithuania or the Ukraine. Set aside for the moment the financial issues of such an endeavor and consider the following questions: Are you familiar with the history and culture of these areas? Can you speak Lithuanian, Ukrainian, or Russian? Are you prepared to consult with Lithuanian or Ukrainian church leaders to learn whether they are prepared to host and use a group from your church? What contribution will your group make? What counsel have the Lithuanians or Ukrainians offered concerning the kind of help they need? If you go, will you help Lithuanian or Ukrainian believers do their work? Will you be there as co-laborers under their direction, or will you be there to show them how "we do it in America"? More to the point, will you plan the trip because you want to serve or because the exotic location will generate mission interest in your church? Will you go as Christian experts, tourists, or servants? Will you be there to help them or will you be an unnecessary burden on them? Likewise, what do you know about the Orthodox Church and the Roman Catholic Church in Eastern Europe? Do you see their faithful members as Christian sisters and brothers, or do you regard them as legitimate targets for evangelization?[5] Finally, how will your group prepare themselves for the mission? These are merely a few of the questions to answer before embarking on a mission trip.

The interest of Christians in the United States in visiting Eastern Europe is understandable, but "mission trips" to these countries or anywhere else require careful consideration and thorough planning. Consultation with experienced and knowledgeable persons in the United States as well as with the churches and their leaders there is essential.

What About the "Old" Mission Fields?

Missionaries are still working in many countries in Asia, Africa, and Latin America—even in countries such as Nigeria, Japan, and Brazil—where Baptists and others began preaching and planting churches a century or more ago. Though the historic denominations have only token missionary presence in most of these countries, Southern Baptists and other evangelical groups are there in large numbers.

One of the earliest geographical regions entered by Christian missionaries is the Balkan peninsula, which today includes Bosnia, Serbia, Croatia, Montenegro, Albania, Macedonia, Bulgaria, and Greece. Likewise, few continents have received more foreign missionaries—Catholic, Orthodox, and Protestant—than Africa. What has happened in these areas where the church was planted centuries ago and professing Christians number in the millions?

Ethnic and religious strife

Long-simmering hatreds and resentments in Eastern Europe and in eastern and central Africa have the last decade erupted in widespread ferocious ethnic conflict and acts of violence. Why so suddenly? For half a century, communist dictatorships in Eastern Europe suppressed most of the historic ethnic tensions and hatreds that had divided the peoples of Yugoslavia, Armenia, and other republics for centuries. It is now clear that these resentments were not forgotten, but simply seethed under the surface. With the collapse of the Soviet empire and the disintegration of the Yugoslav republic, the long-held rancor and the intense thirst for revenge suddenly exploded in barbarous ethnic wars. An enforced peace currently exists, but the underlying causes of the conflicts remain. Some of those causes are religious.

In East Africa, inter-tribal animosities recently resulted in unimaginable and horrific acts of genocide in Rwanda and Burundi. Lesser conflicts have raged in Somalia and Sudan. Civil strife, often rooted in old tribal enmities, has led to civil wars in Zaire, Angola, Uganda, and Liberia. Even now strife is destabilizing governments in Nigeria, Sierra Leone, and Congo.

To those who know Christian history, the sobering fact is that many of these ethnic hatreds and atrocities were committed not by pagans or "unreached people groups," but by ethnic populations who professed Christianity. This raises, therefore, serious questions not only about evangelization of the animists and Muslims in these areas, but more about the need for re-evangelization of the so-called Christians.

Changing Economies

From the middle of the last century until 1989, socialism and Marxism served as restraints on or alternatives to unbridled capitalism. With the collapse of the Soviet Union, such alternatives are no longer viable. Former socialist economies are being steadily altered, and Marxism survives only in modified form in China and Cuba. Meanwhile, efforts to "reform" the economic systems in numerous countries are imposing indescribable hardships on millions of people, especially on the poor. In Russia, for example, the switch from a planned or controlled economy to a "free market" system has brought the country to the brink of total economic collapse. So widespread is the economic discontent and disillusionment resulting from the failures of the once-touted free-market economy that the Russian government is tottering and there is growing fear of the breakdown of civil restraints. How a total meltdown of the Russian economy or an overthrow of the government would affect mission work in Eastern Europe or how long outsiders can go and come unrestricted is not clear. The likelihood of conditions remaining as they are is at best questionable.

The economy of most African nations is a modified form of capitalism, but the endemic poverty intensified by population growth and huge and mounting foreign debt are contributing to increasing social unrest, crime, governmental corruption, and violence.

What Happened to What We Once Thought and Did?

Customs and traditions—social, political, philosophical, religious, and ethical—generally accepted in times past, particularly in the west, no longer claim universal support. Some say there is no longer a recognized common truth, and the Church has been marginalized. Whether there ever was universal acceptance of "common truth" is debatable. But the privileges, prestige, and influence the Church once enjoyed in the west have diminished as societies have become more secular and culturally and religiously pluralistic. This cultural transformation resulted in what appears to be widespread cynicism. Claims to absolute truth by any religious group, therefore, are disputed and Pilate's question, "What is truth?" seems to epitomize the attitude of growing numbers in the west, especially among young people.

Effects on the Church and on Missions

The Church has not escaped the impact of these changes. Theological beliefs that once characterized and distinguished denominations have less meaning today. Families and individuals move from church to church and from denomination to denomination with little or no thought regarding the history of these institutions, what they represent theologically, or what they profess to believe. Decisions about which church to join, for example, are based less on theological convictions and more on social and pragmatic reasons. Few concern themselves about the history of a church or denomination, much less with what that church believed or taught generations ago. The erosion of "brand loyalty" in purchasing patterns is seen no less in the erosion of denominational allegiance. In the United States, the divisions in Protestantism are far more about social and political issues—abortion, school prayer, church and state, and welfare—than about theological questions such as predestination, the mode of baptism, or the presence of Christ in the Eucharist. This is not to imply that theology no longer divides Christians. Women's ordination, the inerrancy of the Bible, and homosexuality are among issues that have provoked fierce battles in many Christian churches, including the Roman Catholic and Anglican communions, in recent years.

The Southern Baptist Convention is a case in point. Beginning in 1979 Southern Baptists experienced the first onslaught of a reactionary group—theological fundamentalists for the most part—who initiated their well-calculated plan to gain control of the denomination. In less than a decade they dominated every agency and institution owned and operated by the Convention. Though there has not been a major split, hundreds of churches have either left the Convention entirely or have been pushed to the margins of the denomination.

Fifty years ago the Sunday School Board was the single publication house for Southern Baptists. Four seminaries—Southern, Southwestern, New Orleans, and Golden Gate—were scattered across the country. Two others have been added since, Southeastern in 1951 and Midwestern in 1958. In 1948 Southern Baptists had two mission boards: the Foreign Mission Board in Richmond and the Home Mission Board in Atlanta. The denomination was tightly knit and loyalty was measured by support of these institutions through the Cooperative Program and the annual mission offerings.

Today many once loyal Southern Baptist churches buy their literature from one or more of six publication houses. Theological students can choose from 18 Baptist seminaries and divinity schools,[6] and there are multiple mission agencies and para-church groups competing for Baptist money. Denominational loyalty is no longer a given. In fact, for many Baptists it is an option while for others it is an anachronism. This is not a phenomenon limited to Baptists. It is a growing problem in most denominations. The divisions in the SBC and the new movements and institutions resulting mirror unprecedented changes going on in churches everywhere.

These are only a few of the more obvious changes that have affected the Church and mission today. How each congregation reacts varies, of course, but none is totally immune from what is happening.

Notes

[1] The term "Third World" originated in the 1950s and referred to those countries in Asia, Africa, and Latin America, which, theoretically, were neither a part of the communist nor the non-communist blocs. Most of them, nonetheless, were influenced and some dominated by one bloc or the other. Subsequently, the term "Third World" became a designation for the economically under-developed or poorest of the world's nations. Because they represented approximately two-thirds of the world's population, they eventually came to be known as the "Two-Thirds World."

[2] The very conservative Jewish Orthodox can exercise so much influence because Israel has more than two dozen political parties, none of which has ever won an outright majority. The party with the largest plurality therefore is forced to make deals and concessions with others if they are to form a coalition government. The Orthodox representatives in the government thereby consistently hold the balance of power and, therefore, are able to exert inordinate influence. The result is a kind of religious freedom, but it is at best a limited freedom.

[3] This post-denominationalism, which is imposed from the outside, is not universal. The Seventh Day Adventists and the Little Flock are registered with the government and legally hold worship services in their own buildings and attract large numbers of believers.

[4] The term "house church" usually refers to those groups not legally registered. Legally registered groups not recognized as "churches" are called "Christian meeting points."

[5] A few years ago I attended a meeting with a number of church leaders from Romania, Bosnia, and Russia. Three of the delegates from Moscow reported that at least four hundred different Protestant and evangelical groups had rented offices in the Russian capital and were bringing in hundreds of short-term evangelists and other religious groups. The delegates added that this burgeoning presence was creating significant problems for the churches. Not only did the Orthodox deeply resent the implications that non-evangelicals are not Christians, but even some of the evangelical congregations were being overwhelmed with requests for hosting these short-term missioners.

[6] Besides the six SBC seminaries, there are the Richmond, Baylor, Central, Mid-America, Luther Rice, and Criswell seminaries, plus Baptist divinity schools at Gardner Webb, Campbell, Wake Forest, Mercer, Samford, and Hardin-Simmons universities. Also, there are Baptist Houses of Study at Duke Divinity, Emory University's Candler Divinity, and Texas Christian University's Brite Divinity schools.

"During the colonial era, Christian writers presented Western missionaries in a totally positive light. Later anticolonial writers painted them as servants of colonialism and destroyers of cultures. In recent years, historians... have begun to reinterpret mission history from a global perspective. They see both the good and the bad in the modern mission movement, and recognize that, despite its weaknesses, the movement did plant the church throughout the world. Globalization, however, not only changes how we view missions but also how we do it."

- Paul G. Hiebert, *Missiological Implications of Epistemological Shifts* (1999).

Chapter 2

Mission Yesterday, Today, and Tomorrow

From 1706 when the first Protestant missionaries arrived in Tranquebar, the Danish colony on the southeast shore of India, until the end of the Second World War in 1945, Protestant mission work was a European and later a North American endeavor. Missions were financed by churches and individuals, and virtually all the missionaries sent to Asia, Africa, and Latin America were either Europeans or North Americans. The missionaries were in charge of the "native" workers, the churches, schools, hospitals, and other mission institutions.

Initially transportation to and from the mission fields was slow, often taking months to get to the destination. Even as late as the 1950s travel to the "field" was a voyage of many days or weeks. Moreover, missionaries could enter most non-Christian lands without concern about passports or visas, primarily because most of these lands were colonies of western empires. During the early colonial era missionaries were required to secure permission from private European companies, such as the British East India Company, to travel on a British ship and to live or work in a British colony. Eventually, however, this became little more than a formality.

What Happened?

Roman Catholics had been sending missionaries to various parts of the world since the end of the sixth century and some eastern Christian churches had sent missionaries even earlier. Prior to the time of William Carey (1761-1834), however, missionary activity among Protestants consisted of efforts made by a few enthusiasts in the Lutheran, Reformed, and Anglican churches. After 1792, however, foreign missions became official denominational undertakings not only in the aforementioned churches, but also among the Baptists, Congregationalists, Presbyterians, and Methodists. In succeeding generations, mission activity and mission promotion became integral and indispensable elements in the growth and vitality of these denominations.

Denominational mission bodies, however, were joined by a growing number of non-denominational missionary agencies such as the London Missionary Society founded in 1795 (three years after Carey's group organized the Baptist mission society[1]) and the China Inland Mission founded in 1865. Today there are hundreds of Protestant and evangelical missionary-sending agencies in the United States and Canada, plus hundreds more in other countries.[2]

With the exception of Southern Baptists most of the historic denominations, such as the Methodists, Presbyterians, Episcopalians, and Roman Catholics, are commissioning significantly fewer foreign missionaries than they did a generation or two ago. Many factors contribute to the diminishing numbers, and the lower numbers do not necessarily indicate a loss of mission interest or a lack of concern for people in other parts of the world.

Despite the changes that have occurred in the kind and level of mission involvement by the historic denominations, the following appear to be clear:

- It is increasingly difficult to recruit vocational missionaries who are willing to spend their lives in another land and another culture.

- The speed and relatively modest economic costs of traveling abroad make it easy for Christians in the west and elsewhere to be short-term volunteers or missionaries. These Christians can often arrange trips directly with national Christian leaders and thus avoid waiting for or depending on approval by a mission agency in the United States.

- Mission boards, especially the larger ones, are struggling to remain serious players in the context of a rapidly evolving missionary entrepreneurship by individuals and congregations. A generation ago no Southern Baptist, for example, would have thought about going to Kenya or Brazil without soliciting the approval and assistance of the Foreign Mission Board. Furthermore, the Board set and oversaw the policy for mission involvement overseas by SBC congregations or individuals. Now the Board is more a facilitator of what the churches and church groups decide to do unilaterally.

- Pastors and members now want to be participants in mission, not merely supporters. "Hands-on" experience excites them and revitalizes their people. As a result the congregation is prompted to intensify their direct involvement in mission, both nationally and internationally.[3]

- Local churches are no longer dependent on or willing to wait for denominational bureaucracies to approve or make arrangements for them. Many congregations are large enough or venturesome enough to initiate and carry out their own mission projects, thereby bypassing the denominational mission agencies altogether.[4]

- Though these developments have forced the mission agencies to alter their traditional roles, the number of grassroots Christians involved in the world mission of the Church has increased dramatically.

- At the same time there is no indication that the number of mission organizations and agencies is shrinking or that their continuation is endangered. In fact, besides the long-established mission boards and agencies of the Protestant and evangelical denominations and the older non-denominational mission societies, there are hundreds of newer independent and para-church groups doing missions in various parts of the world. Some send career and/or short-term missionaries, but many simply provide economic and other forms of aid to national Christian churches and individuals in other parts of the world.[5]

- In addition to the mission agencies functioning in western Europe, North America, Australia, and New Zealand, hundreds of new missionary-sending groups have sprung up during the past twenty years in countries that until the 1960s *received* missionaries, such as Korea, Japan, India, Brazil, and Nigeria. For example, today one can find Japanese Christian missionaries living and working in Brazil, Korean missionaries in Chile and Ghana, Brazilian missionaries in Angola and Mozambique, and Nigerian missionaries in Chad and Cameroon as well as in St. Paul and Minneapolis.[6] Churches in the "Third World" are not only increasingly assuming responsibility for the evangelization of their own people, but many of them are sending missionaries to other lands including the United States and Canada. No one knows precisely the number of these "Third World" mission-sending bodies, but it is certain that there are hundreds of them.

- Equally significant is the fact that the migration of non-Christian peoples to the west is at an all-time high. Also, though the majority of Hindus still are in India, there are millions in the West—2,000, for example, in the Research Triangle of North Carolina alone. The same can be said of Muslims, Buddhists, Sikhs, Jains, Zoroastrians, and others. Thus, if one is truly interested in doing mission work among one or more of these religious groups, the place to begin is in one's own city or town.

We are truly living in a much different world today, and we face conditions and challenges our forebears never encountered.

What Are the Risks?

Given the increase in ethnic violence and international terrorism, is it any more dangerous to be a missionary now than in previous generations? Probably not. Occasionally one hears of a missionary's being kidnapped or killed, but these are isolated and infrequent occurrences. A missionary is far more likely to be killed or seriously hurt in an automobile accident than as a victim of violence. Compared with the loss of life in the Boxer Rebellion in China in 1900 when 165 missionaries and 134 missionary children were killed, the current loss of missionary life due to violence is minimal.[7]

What Are the Current Issues and Challenges?

The percentage of the world that is non-Christian has hardly changed in the last half-century, but of the 5.8 billion people in the world, at least 20 percent have little or no exposure to the gospel. Many are what some evangelical missiologists call "unreached" or the "hidden" peoples, and most of them will not hear the gospel unless someone goes to them with the gospel.

The question is, "Who should go?" Should we send large numbers of missionaries from the United States or other western countries to these remote and isolated areas, given that the costs average $75,000 per missionary couple per year? Should we encourage Christians from the west to enter China or Cambodia, for example, pretending to be teachers or otherwise, an illegal and potentially dangerous practice?

Why not depend primarily on short-term missionary personnel? After all, it is so much easier to attract people for short-term mission activities than for long-term career or vocational work. The vast majority of "missionaries" today go for a week to a month to two years, not for a decade or several decades as they did in the past. One need not and should not minimize or denigrate the good that some of the short-term missioners do or the impact these experiences make on them and the congregations from which they come. This is the credit side of the ledger. Too often, however, sincere people go on a "mission trip" knowing little if anything about the history, culture, or language of the people to whom they go. Rarely can they communicate in any language other than English, and rarely are they there long enough to know the people, much less learn the language or become involved—genuinely involved—in the peoples' lives.

If communicating the gospel involves nothing more than an auditory exercise, then traveling briefly to another land and "preaching the gospel" through an interpreter may be enough. But communicating the gospel involves doing what Jesus did: "...he became flesh and lived among us." (John 1:14)

Emphasis on evangelism and church planting is currently so popular that most of the larger missionary-sending bodies are inclined to do little else. Moreover, they manifest minimal and sometimes no interest in what may be called comprehensive or holistic missions such as educational, medical, agricultural, or social ministries. As a consequence, many of the institutions founded by the early missionaries now suffer from critical shortages of personnel—particularly from a shortage of funds.

The International Baptist Theological Seminary in Cali, Colombia, is a good example. Built in the early 1950s on a twenty-five acre plot, the Seminary decided to sell part of the unused property for a housing development in the 1970s. The FMB allowed the Seminary to keep only a part of the proceeds for endowment. Now the Seminary must function without the steady inflow of money from Richmond and with no missionary personnel. The same is true for scores of institutions around the world.

The current de-emphasis on comprehensive missions suggests a widespread ignoring of the fact that more than a billion people in the world live without the most basic necessities—adequate food, potable water, housing fit for human occupation, and steady, meaningful work. These individuals lack access to medical care. They lack protection from violence and exploitation and are victims of incredibly unjust and inhuman social and political systems.

The number of refugees—persons who must flee their homes and their lands—has increased steadily since the early 1950s, fluctuating between 50 and 100 million. Rather than being welcomed and protected, many countries, including the United States, imprison them and repatriate them as quickly as possible.

The most shameful situation, truly an international scandal, is the number of children (at least 100 million; 200 million according to the UN) who literally live on the street. If they survive, they do so without parental guidance or protection, extended families, education, or physical, emotional, or social safeguards of any kind. No major city in this country is without its share of homeless persons, many being street children. Peruse Phyllis Kilbourn's *Street Children: A Guide to Effective Ministry*[8] for an idea of the mammoth dimensions of this problem.

Why are some of us willing to give money to send missionaries to other lands when we have so many lost, abused, and exploited children in our own land? Moreover, can we rest easy knowing that larger and more grand church buildings are being constructed here and for example, in Brazil when hundreds of thousands of children in both countries have no decent or safe place to sleep tonight?

Finally, the gap between the rich and the poor of the world, even in our own country, increases daily. In July 1998 it was reported that the wealth of Bill Gates, CEO of Microsoft Corporation, exceeds the combined resources of 106 million U.S. citizens. Most of us Christians in the west have far more than we actually need while a billion or more people in other parts of the world have little or nothing. Read again Matthew 25:31-46 and ask yourself, "What are the mission implications of what Jesus said?"

What Does This Signify for the Church Tomorrow?

We have entered a new century. This may mean little more than turning the pages of a calendar, but it does give us opportunity to reflect on the past as well as the present, to consider what we are now and what we should be in the future. I have mentioned only the most obvious conditions related to the doing of mission, and I am not speaking for any group or as an authority. I simply am a concerned believer who sees many congregations floundering and wondering if they still have a mission. To these I would affirm the following: *The world today, as much as any time in history, needs churches who understand and are committed to the work and the gospel of Jesus Christ.* Please do not understand me to be saying that we need to go back and do mission as it was done in the past. The way mission was done in previous centuries grew out of the way the world was at that time. Because the world has changed, we need to learn to think differently and do things differently.

Who will be our model? Is there anyone in the past who can serve as a model for us as we face the future?

A Simple Exercise

Can you arrange six common "kitchen matches" so they form four equilateral triangles? Keep in mind, to do so you have to think differently.[9]

Notes

[1] Originally it was called "The Particular Baptist Society for Propagating the Gospel Among the Heathen," and later was known as "The Baptist Missions Society."

[2] According to the Mission Advance Research Center (MARC) in Monrovia, California, there are some 750 agencies in the United States and Canada that in one way or another are involved internationally in missions. Most are quite modest in size and budget, but some send hundreds of vocational missionaries each year and thousands of short-term personnel and volunteers.

[3] See Appendix A.

[4] See Paul E. Pierson, "Local Churches in Mission: What's Behind the Impatience with Traditional Mission Agencies." *International Bulletin of Missionary Research* 22 (October 1998) 146-150.

[5] See W. Dayton Roberts and John A. Siewert, *Mission Handbook* (Monrovia, CA: MARC, 1989) 57. Researchers for MARC discovered 26 new mission agencies founded in the United States between 1985 and 1987. Most of theses agencies had budgets of less than $200,000 a year.

[6] See "Out of Africa," in the Minneapolis *Star Tribune* (June 20, 1998) B1, 8. The article begins: "Christianity in Africa is on fire, and missionaries from churches there are bringing the flame of the Holy Spirit to this country. They are returning the re-energized and reinvigorated faith brought to them generations ago from America and Europe."

[7] See G. Thompson Brown, *Earthen Vessels & Transcendent Power* (Orbis, 1997) 156. The Boxer Uprising resulted in severe losses for the church in northern China. Some estimate that 30,000 Chinese Roman Catholics and 1,900 Chinese Protestants lost their lives in addition to five bishops, 31 European priests, and nine sisters. Protestant missionaries put to death numbered 134 plus 52 of their children. The most significant loss of missionaries to violence since 1900 occurred in Latin America between 1952 and 1990, mostly at the hands of right-wing military and paramilitary groups.

[8] See Phyllis Kilbourn, *Street Children: A Guide to Effective Ministry* (Monrovia, CA: MARC, 1997).

[9] Think three-dimensionally. Arrange the matches to form a pyramid.

"We know now that God is like this that we have seen in Jesus. God is Christlike. And if God is Christlike, God is good and trustable.... Strange, a man lived among us, and when we think of God we must think of God in terms of this person, or God is not good. ...we may transfer every single moral quality in Jesus to God without loss or degradation to our thoughts of God. On the contrary, by thinking of God in terms of Jesus we heighten our view of God."

—E. Stanley Jones , The Christ of Every Road (1931).

Chapter 3

A Model for Doing Mission

Most of us are aware of Christian congregations where there is little or no sense of mission. Either the passion for mission has dissipated completely or it is barely a flicker. In the final chapter of this book, some remedies for this common malady will be suggested. To prevent, however, is easier than to cure. One of the first steps therefore to enhancing a church's sense of mission is to agree on a missionary model.

In the early 1930s Swiss theologian H. Emil Brunner wrote a little book that was translated into English under the title *The Word and the World*.[1] In this small volume Brunner said, "The church exists by mission, just as fire exists by burning." Few, if any, declarations about mission have been so influential, so widely quoted as this concise description of the relation of mission to the life of the church. Without combustion, Brunner declared, there is no fire, and without mission there is no church. There may be a beautiful building, a convivial fellowship, a thriving and prosperous organization—a club as it were—but if there is no consciousness of being sent, and no implementation of being sent into the world, there is no church in the New Testament or Christian sense of mission.

Jürgen Moltman agreed a half-century later when he observed "mission does not come from the church; it is from mission and in the light of mission that the church has to be understood."[2] Mission is not the result of the church. The church is the result of mission. The earliest evidence is the New Testament itself. The twenty-seven documents that we call the

Christian Scriptures were written for a church on mission. They are, above anything else, essentially missionary documents.

"Whom would you choose as an ideal model for the doing of mission in the next decade or next century?" Responses to that question by a class or a congregation often range from what other churches are doing to what the denomination recommends. When I pose the question to groups or individuals I look for something more basic, such as an individual missionary. When this is made clear, the names of familiar missionaries are mentioned: Lottie Moon, David Livingstone, William Carey, Adoniram and Ann Judson, Henrietta Hall Shuck, Ida Scudder, and E. Stanley Jones. Certainly we can benefit from studying the lives of these and hundreds of other missionaries. However, for a model or pattern, should we not go back to the earliest Christian missionaries?

Years ago I heard Dr. Josef Nordenhaug, then General Secretary of the Baptist World Alliance, tell of an experience he had as a boy. He said he was helping his cabinetmaker father in his shop:

> One day my father handed me a length of board. "Son, cut me seven pieces the length of this one." It was not a difficult assignment, or so I thought. I laid the length of board my father gave me on top of the first board I was to cut. I marked the length carefully and I sawed the end off of what was the first of seven pieces. Then I took the piece I had just cut and laid it on top of the third piece. I again marked the length carefully and cut it as I had done the first time. I repeated this procedure until I had cut all seven pieces. Then I proudly stood them up to hand them to my father and made a startling discovery. The pieces I had cut were not the same length as the piece my father had given me. In fact, each was shorter than the previous piece. And though the first piece I cut was only slightly shorter than the piece my father had given me, each piece was shorter than the preceding one. The seventh piece was noticeably so. They were shorter because I had failed to use for each measurement the board my father had given to me.[3]

If we are going to have a model or pattern by which we engage in mission, should we not go back to the original? Who should be considered the original? Frequently when I ask this question someone responds, "The Apostle Paul." He's not a bad choice, but I suggest we consider first Jesus as our model.

A.

Jesus as Our Model for Mission

To think of Jesus as a missionary may be a new concept for many. Consider: the words "mission" and "missionary" come from the root meaning *to send* or *to be sent.* Has there been anyone in Christian history who manifested more of a consciousness of being sent than Jesus? When he began his public ministry in Nazareth, he was given the scroll of the prophet Isaiah, and he read: "The Spirit of the Lord is upon me, because God has sent me to bring good news to the poor" (Luke 4:18). Following the memorable declaration in the Gospel of John that "God so loved the world that God gave his only son," the writer adds: "Indeed, God did not send the Son into the world to condemn the world, but in order that the world might be saved through him" (4:16, 17). If there has ever been a person with a sense of mission, it was Jesus. His mission determined and defined his vocation.

We begin with Jesus for two important reasons. First, because Jesus discloses to us what God is like. In his book *The Christ of Every Road,* E. Stanley Jones states that Jesus is crucial because in him we get a full picture of what God is like:

> We know now that God is like this that we have seen in Jesus. God is Christlike. And if God is Christlike, God is good and trustable.... Strange, a man lived among us, and when we think of God we must think of God in terms of this person, or God is not good. ...We may transfer every single moral quality in Jesus to God without loss or degradation to our thought of God. On the contrary, by thinking of God in terms of Jesus we heighten our view of God.[4]

Moreover, we can only understand the motive for and dimensions of the Christian mission by looking carefully at the mission of Jesus.

Choose one of the Gospels—Mark, for example—and read quickly through it. If you are in a group, assign the chapters to certain individuals, and ask them to make notes about the ministry of Jesus. How would you describe it from what you read?

The Mission and Ministry of Jesus as He Defined Them

On more than one occasion Jesus described the purpose of his life and ministry. To his disciples he said on one occasion:

> You know that among the Gentiles those whom they recognize as their rulers lord it over them, and their great ones are tyrants over them. But it is not so among you; but whoever wishes to become great among you must be your servant, and whoever wishes to be first among you must be slave of all. For the Son of Man came not to be served but to serve, and to give his life a ransom for many. (Mark 10:42-45)

Jesus' purpose was not to save institutions. It was not to acquire prestige, power, or wealth. His mission was to serve those who were in need—"the lost," as he described them. He illustrated this by his emphasis on love for one's neighbor, forgiveness of one's enemies, and being willing to do the most humble tasks. At the beginning of the last week of his life, Jesus provided a vivid example by washing his disciples' feet and bidding them to do likewise, to exemplify that same kind of servant attitude and action.

Surprisingly, he said the whole of the commandments—all ten of them—could be summed up in two: undivided love for God and unconditional love for one's neighbor. Jesus depicted this love for neighbor with the story of the Samaritan who, unlike the priest and the teacher of the law, did not ignore or avoid a man wounded and left for dead. The Samaritan did not rest with merely summoning help. He did not limit his participation simply to protesting the violence occurring on the road to Jericho. Rather, this Samaritan made the victim his neighbor and assumed an ongoing responsibility and concern for him. Reflecting on the story as Jesus told it reveals a person, the Samaritan in this case, who identified with, had compassion for, and became directly involved in the life of the victim.

Jesus, however, did not claim that his ministry was unique. In fact, he openly identified with John the Baptist. Jesus sanctioned John's life and work, and he indicated that their lives and efforts were directly related. Moreover, Jesus called others—disciples—to apprentice with him and to reproduce or replicate his ministry.

Jesus began his ministry in Nazareth by declaring that he was called to bring good news to the poor, proclaim release to the captives and recovery of sight to the blind, to let the oppressed go free, [and] proclaim the year of the Lord's favor (Luke 4:18-19). What would constitute good news to the poor? Would it have been that there was a spiritual blessing awaiting them sometime in the distant future? Hardly. The good news was that their poverty would soon end, the slaves and prisoners would be freed, the blind would see, and oppression would cease because the year of Jubilee was at hand. What would happen in the Jubilee year? All debts would be canceled, all slaves would be liberated, and all alienated land would be returned to its original owners.

Jesus' mission literalized and historicized the good news by healing men, women, and children—the lame, the blind, the physically deformed, the chronically ill, the "possessed"; by feeding the hungry; by including in his community many who were socially and religiously ostracized; and by restoring the dead to life. Jesus even insisted that children be permitted access to him. All four gospels record these things.

The Mission and Ministry of Jesus as Described by the Gospels

Following his baptism, Jesus went to the desert, the place where he occasionally retreated to pray and to prepare for and resist the incessant temptations to abandon his mission and settle for something less.

Often Jesus was in the Temple or the synagogues, but he did not limit his ministry to religious shrines or places. He also preached and taught in the market places, in the streets and in the fields, and in the peoples' houses. His mission included both teaching and preaching. Do you know the difference, and can you give an example of each?

On more than one occasion Jesus violated customs and ignored religious rules, such as healing people on the Sabbath. His behavior and his insistence that the welfare of individuals was far more important than observing religious codes frequently aroused questions, suspicion, and intense criticism. When Jesus healed the sick on the Sabbath and when he declared people forgiven of their sins, such as the paralyzed man brought by his four friends, opposition increased dramatically.

Clearly Jesus did remarkable things—miracles—but he did not perform on demand. When some of the religious leaders challenged him to demonstrate his power by doing a miracle, he flatly refused. His phenomenal works were never done to call attention to himself or to enhance himself in the eyes of the people. They were acts of love and compassion, not sensational feats to attract crowds.

Despite the fact that the religious system was in many respects corrupt, Jesus frequented the synagogues and the Temple in Jerusalem. He denounced, however, those religious leaders who sought privilege and recognition rather than serving the poor and protecting the defenseless, such as widows and children, from exploitation. In fact, Jesus condemned those rabbis and "teachers of the Law" who used their positions to "rob" widows of their houses and oppress the poor. Jesus was dedicated to protecting the weak, healing the sick, and restoring the ostracized and the fallen to a place in the community. For example, his teaching on divorce was to protect women of his time who had few rights and no social or political power, not to victimize them further with legalistic condemnation. Though Jesus condemned hypocrisy in the strongest terms, he never rejected anyone who came to him with honest questions, such as the rich young ruler.

Early in his ministry, according to the gospels, Jesus saw the likelihood of his impending clash with the religious leaders. He used his forthcoming suffering and death to explain to his disciples the meaning of discipleship. Any ministry, therefore, that represents the Christian life as one of assured prosperity or devoid of failure and pain is not in keeping with what Jesus taught about discipleship.

Jesus did not do nor did he try to do his work alone. Repeatedly he sent his disciples out to teach, preach, and heal, and his final words to them were a commission—a fascinating word meaning to bring together those on mission. The commission directly linked them to himself as the one who was sending them into the world:

> All authority in heaven and on earth has been given to me. Go therefore and make disciples of all ethnic groups, baptizing them in the name of the Father and of the Son and of the Holy Spirit, and teaching them to obey everything that I have commanded you. (Matthew 28:18-20)

Frequently when pastors and other church leaders talk about Christ's commission to his disciples emphasis is placed on the word translated "Go." However, the term can also be translated "as you go" or "as you are going." Human beings have been on the move since the beginning of the human race. Christ's imperative therefore is not to go, but to disciple, baptize, and teach what Jesus taught.

Summarize the Mission and Ministry of Jesus

____

____

____

____

____

____

____

____

____

Paul as Our Model for Mission

Scholars generally agree that the earliest documents, which subsequently became integral segments of what Christians call the New Testament, were letters attributed to the Apostle Paul. In fact, these thirteen letters represent more than one-fifth of the New Testament.[5] Not only did Paul write much of the New Testament, but he was a major force in moving the Christian community from being a reformed branch of Judaism to being an inclusive world church. How can we account for this?

Paul's Conversion and Subsequent Involvement in Mission

According to Paul's own testimony, he received the gospel not from any person, nor was he formally instructed in the fine points of the Christian faith by the church. Rather, Paul declared, the gospel was revealed directly to him by Jesus Christ (Gal 1:11-12). Some might wonder how this could happen to a faithful follower of Judaism, and Paul makes it clear that he was not on the margins of Judaism at the time of his conversion. At the time his life was so radically and dramatically changed he was a leader in the persecution of the followers of Christ. He was on his way to Damascus of Syria to arrest all the followers of Jesus he could find when God stopped and arrested him. This was no impromptu event, Paul said, for it was "by God's grace I was chosen to serve, even before I was born. It was because God had destined me to proclaim the Good News about Jesus Christ to the Gentiles that God revealed Jesus to me" (Gal 1:15-16).

Though he was later commissioned by the church in Antioch of Syria to accompany Barnabas on their first missionary journey, Paul never wavered in his insistence that his initial commission was from God. After the Damascus road experience, Paul insisted, he did not consult anyone, nor did he go to Jerusalem to seek the Apostles' approval.

"Instead, I went at once to Arabia, and then I returned to Damascus. It was three years later that I went to Jerusalem to get information from Peter, and I stayed with him for two weeks. I did not see any other apostle except James, the Lord's brother" (Gal 1:17b-19 TEV). This is all that Paul says about his visit to Jerusalem. The account in Acts, however, is more revealing. It implies that Paul was not immediately accepted by the Jerusalem church. They were afraid of him, and they found it hard to believe that his profession of faith was genuine. A leader in the church, Barnabas, vouched for him by telling the church how Paul had been changed and how courageously he had witnessed about Jesus while he was in Damascus. Reading between the lines, however, one can readily draw the conclusion that despite the assurances by Barnabas, Paul had a way to go before he was able to convince the Jerusalem church of his sincerity. Paul had been there only a matter of days when a plot to kill him was uncovered. At that point some of the brothers of the church took Paul to the port at Caesarea and put him on a boat bound for Tarsus (Acts 9:1-30).

Whether Paul would have reemerged in the history of Christianity had he not later been enlisted by Barnabas to come to Antioch of Syria, we have no way of knowing. Apparently Barnabas saw what was happening in the Antioch congregation. He saw the possibility of incorporating Paul into the work in this new Jewish-Gentile congregation. So Barnabas journeyed to Tarsus, convinced Paul that he was needed, and both of them returned to Antioch and became key leaders in the church. It was this church, not the congregation in Jerusalem, that commissioned Barnabas and Paul for their first missionary journey.

Paul's Missionary Approach as Gleaned from the Acts of the Apostles and Paul's Letters

Usually Paul would begin in a synagogue by seeking to convince the Jewish faithful as well as Jewish proselytes[6] and God-fearers[7] that Jesus was the promised Messiah. He preached, taught, discussed, and even debated. The essence of his preaching was that:

> God the Creator chose our ancestors, and made of them a numerous people while they were in Egypt, and because of their population growth and influence, they were enslaved. But God freed our forebears from Egyptian bondage, made them a great nation, and promised to send a Messiah or Savior.
>
> Jesus of Nazareth was that Messiah. But he was rejected by his own people, and eventually he was arrested and cruelly executed.
>
> The good news is that God raised Jesus from death, and it is through faith in him, not by trying to live according to the Law of Moses, that our sins are forgiven and we are made right with God.

Herein lay the core of the gospel for the Jews, according to Paul, but like the contemporaries of Jesus, Paul's Jewish hearers often rejected his message. Some Jews, however, along with many God-fearers and other Gentiles, accepted the Apostle's words as truth. These were baptized and formed by Paul into Christian communities or churches. Positive response to his preaching and teaching frequently resulted in physical attacks on Paul and his companions. In Lystra, Derbe, Philippi, and Ephesus, for example, Paul came dangerously close to being killed.

Unlike Jesus', Paul's was not a holistic or comprehensive ministry. On one occasion, in Lystra, he healed a crippled man, which led to his and Barnabas' being mistaken for the Greek gods Zeus and Hermes (Acts 14:8-18). On his way back to Jerusalem at the end of his second missionary journey, Paul restored Eutychus to life (Acts 20:7-12). Paul took relief money to the suffering believers in Judea on at least two occasions. There is, however, no indication that Paul ever started schools or opened medical clinics. Apparently, he was concerned with neither the causes or resolutions of poverty nor the widespread oppression of slaves.[8] It appears that he, like everyone else of his time, assumed that poverty was an intractable condition and that slavery was an immutable institution.

Paul was not a social reformer. He was primarily an itinerant evangelist, apparently never remaining long in any one place or staying for extended periods of time with the new and fledgling congregations he began. Before leaving them, however, he seems always to have named "elders" to shepherd them. We have no accurate count as to how many churches Paul began, nor do we know all the things he did to shape them and later to encourage them. Obviously he wrote them letters, sent colleagues to help them, and revisited at least some of them from time to time. He did not, however, attempt to administer these congregations, nor did he assume any financial responsibility for them. On two occasions at least—as already noted—Paul took relief money to help the poor in Judea.[9] Other than these times, there is no indication that he carried or sent money to any other congregation.

One of the earliest and most stirring statements on Christian stewardship is found in Paul's second letter to the church at Corinth. He praises the sacrificial giving of the churches in Macedonia to help the poor in Judea—Jewish poor that the Macedonian believers did not know and likely would never see (8:1-9:15). The underlying reason for such Christian compassion, Paul said, was gratitude. "For you there in Corinth know the grace of our Lord Jesus Christ, though he was rich, for your sake he became poor, that through his poverty you might be made rich" (8:9). Paul insisted that he himself never received pay for his missionary work, taking pride instead in the fact that he was able to support himself by his previously practiced trade, tent-making. In his final meeting with the elders of the church in Ephesus Paul said:

> You yourselves know that I have worked with my own hands and provided everything that my companions and I have needed. I have shown you in all things that by working hard in this way we must help the weak, remembering the words that the Lord Jesus himself said, "It is more blessed to give than to receive." (Acts 20:34-35)

Paul was not, however, without flaws. His unwillingness to give John Mark a second chance ended Paul's relationship with Barnabas, a schism evidently provoked by Paul's rigidity and refusal to allow Mark to accompany the two missionaries on their second journey. Paul also was highly critical of those who insisted that Gentile believers submit to the rite of circumcision. Yet after Paul separated from Barnabas, Paul circumcised young Timothy prior to taking him as a missionary colleague. Paul's views on marriage expressed to the church in Corinth (1 Cor 7:1-16) are troubling to most of us today, and they were significantly less elevated than what is attributed to him in his letter to the church in Ephesus (5:21-32). Furthermore, his comments in various letters about women simply cannot be reconciled, and his views on these thorny issues should not be taken as contemporary directives.[10]

Paul's venture into Greece was the result of not being able to go where he wanted, which evidently led to Paul's vision or dream while in

Troas. In this dream a man of Macedonia urged Paul to cross the Aegean Sea and come to Europe, which he did. Curiously, the first two people he was able to help were women, Lydia and the slave girl (Acts 16:11-19). Paul found no synagogue in Philippi, so on the Sabbath he and his companions went to the nearby river where he expected the Jews to be gathered for prayer. Apparently no men were present, so Paul spoke with the women there. Lydia, a businesswoman, accepted Paul's message and was baptized along with everyone in her household. Whether Paul or one of his colleagues baptized these new believers is not clear.

As on other occasions, Paul accepted the hospitality of Lydia to stay in her home, something he customarily did, and offering hospitality to believers became a common practice among Christians of the early centuries.

When Paul healed the slave girl, her owners were infuriated. They denounced the missionaries to the civil authorities who, in turn, ordered Paul and Silas punished and thrown into jail. The ensuing earthquake and conversion of the Philippian jailer provide an insight into Paul's preaching to non-Jews. When the jailer asked what he had to do to be saved, Paul replied succinctly, "Believe in the Lord Jesus Christ, and you will be saved—you and your entire family" (Acts 16:31). This of course was not all that Paul said to the jailer, as verse 32 indicates. However, the essence of the gospel Paul preached can be summarized in these momentous words, "Believe in the Lord Jesus Christ." The message is straightforward and is stated in a way that the jailer and his family can easily comprehend. It involved much more than mental assent, as the entire account reveals. It involved an affirmation and demonstration of faith by submission to baptism.

Later, in Athens, Paul moved to contextualize the gospel in a more dramatic way. He began his address in the Areopagus by acknowledging the multiple evidences of Greek religious devotion that he could have condemned as unmitigated idolatry. He also chose to say that he can tell them the name of the deity whose shrine they had dedicated "To the Unknown God" (Acts 17:23). Furthermore, Paul sought to connect with his hearers by citing the words of a Greek poet and employing a basic idea of the Greek Stoics:

> God, who made the world and everything in it, is Lord of heaven and earth, and does not live in temples made by human hands. Nor is God in need of anything that human beings can provide, since it is God who gives life and breath and everything else to human beings.... God

> is not far from any of us, for "In him we live and move and are." Or as some of your poets have written, "We are all God's children." (Acts 17:23-28)

Only a few in Athens understood or accepted Paul's message, but those who did apparently became the earliest members of the church there. Two observations are in order. Paul did not limit his mission efforts to walking up and down the street of Athens launching prayer missiles at pagan temples and shrines. Paul did not mock or denounce their blatant idolatry. He engaged the Athenians in dialogue and presented the gospel in words and illustrations with which they could identify.

When Paul returned to Jerusalem after his second missionary tour, James told him that tens of thousands of Jews had become believers (Acts 21:20). James also reported that it was being said that Paul was telling Jews who lived in the Gentile world that they did not have to live by the law of Moses. James further appealed to Paul to defuse this growing problem, and Paul agreed to "perform the ceremony of purification with four faithful Jewish men" to signal that he had not totally repudiated Judaism. Toward the end of the week, however, Paul was arrested in the Temple area. He seized the occasion to defend himself by stressing his Jewishness, telling his hearers of his dramatic conversion and why he had been preaching the gospel to Gentiles (Acts 21:39-22:29). Rather than calming his accusers, Paul's words incited them even more. Instead of being freed, Paul began his prolonged experience as a prisoner of the Roman government.

Since Paul was a Roman citizen he should have been released, but he was not. On the contrary, he was forced to appear before one government official after another. He used these occasions to try to preach the good news to those who were in the position to set him free, but they did not. Finally in desperation Paul made a formal appeal to Caesar, which he as a Roman citizen had the right to do. Though this likely spared him from severe physical punishment at the time as well as from a plot to assassinate him, it resulted in his final missionary journey—to Rome in chains. Even though he was a prisoner, he took advantage of every opportunity to preach the gospel while en route to as well as in residence in Rome.

Though there is a tradition that Paul was ultimately executed, the New Testament documents are silent on this matter.

Describe Paul as a Missionary Model

Two Crucial Questions

We began this chapter with a quotation from Emil Brunner: "A church exists by mission, just as a fire exists by burning." This raises for us two crucial questions:

- Should our model for mission be Jesus or Paul, or should it be Jesus *and* Paul?

- Does your church have an agreed-upon model for mission? If you believe there is such a model or pattern, please cite or describe it. Does it include the substance of the ministry of Jesus and/or Paul? Is the church involved in evangelism, announcing the good news to the poor, as well as in healing the sick, in liberating the oppressed, and in seeking and saving the lost?

Notes

[1] H. Emil Brunner, *The Word and the World* (London: SCM Press, 1931) 108.

[2] *The Church in the Power of the Spirit*, trans. Margaret Kohl (New York: Harper and Row, 1977) 10.

[3] Josef Nordenhaug, sermon, Rio de Janeiro, Brazil, 1960.

[4] E. Stanley Jones, *The Christ of Every Road* (New York: Abingdon, 1930) 67. I have altered Jones's words slightly.

[5] Traditionally thirteen letters have been attributed to the Apostle Paul. Ten of these letters are generally regarded as authentically Pauline: Romans, 1 & 2 Corinthians, Galatians, Ephesians, Philippians, Colossians, 1 & 2 Thessalonians, and Philemon. Many New Testament scholars, however, doubt that Paul wrote what are known as the Pastoral Epistles, that is, 1 & 2 Timothy, and Titus.

[6] A proselyte was a non-Jew who accepted the Jewish faith and submitted to the requirements of the Jewish law, including circumcision for males. They are mentioned several times in the New Testament (Jn 12:20; Acts 6:5; 13:43; and 17:4). The requirement for becoming a proselyte is found in Exodus 12:48.

[7] God-fearers were those who also espoused Judaism as their religion, but for various reasons did not or could not become proselytes. Men such as the Ethiopian eunuch (Acts 8:26-40), who had been castrated, were not accepted as proselytes, nor were individuals who were born illegitimately.

[8] In his letter to Philemon, Paul admonishes the slave owner to regard Onesimus—whom Paul is returning as Philemon's property—as a brother in Christ, doubtless a plea for mercy and humanitarian treatment of the runaway.

[9] After Paul and Barnabas worked for a year in the Antioch church, the congregation there responded to the crisis resulting from a widespread famine and sent money to their Christian brothers and sisters who were living in Judea. The relief money was taken to Jerusalem by Barnabas and Paul (Acts 11:29-30). Much later, when Paul was working in Macedonia, believers there—even though they were very poor, Paul says—"insisted on the privilege of having a part in helping God's people in Judea" (2 Cor 8:4). Paul refers to the remarkable generosity of the Macedonian believers in his letter to the church in Rome. He informs them, "Right now... I am going to Jerusalem in the service of God's people there. For the churches in Macedonia and Greece have freely decided to give an offering to help the poor among God's people in Jerusalem. They themselves decided to do it. But, as a matter of fact, they have an obligation to help those poor; for the Jews shared their spiritual blessing with the Gentiles, and so the Gentiles ought to serve the Jews with their material blessings. When I have finished this task, and have turned over to them the full amount of money that has been raised for them, I shall leave for Spain and visit you on my way there" (Rom 15: 25-28).

[10] Though he wrote to the church in Galatia that in Christ there is no difference between Jew and Greek, male and female, one finds the troubling mandate in 1 Cor 14:34 that women "should keep quiet in the church meetings," not to mention the more inconsistent statement incorrectly attributed to Paul in 1 Timothy 2:12-15.

Part 2

I find myself suspicious of those who continue to define "global" or "borderland" as an overseas event and not one going on right across the street in Newark or Hartford or Los Angeles or New York City. The history of missions in mainline or historic denominations has shown that there is a safety that comes with distance that has been at the core for funding and promoting foreign missions. However when that same missionary work is redirected toward the racial ethnic populations within the country, funding is hard to come by and the work is done mostly as "special ministries" projects that are created to be of short duration.

—Daisy L. Machado, "Latino Church History: A Haunting Memory" (1998).

Chapter 4

An Analysis of the International Mission Board and Its Program

Because the International Mission Board has been doing missions for more than 150 years and has thousands of missionaries under appointment, its strengths and weaknesses are more apparent than those of the much younger and smaller Cooperative Baptist Fellowship and Alliance of Baptists.

The Foreign Mission Board, now known as the International Mission Board, was established in 1845, one of the principal actions taken during the founding meeting of the Southern Baptist Convention in Augusta, Georgia.[1] The twofold purpose of the Board is to serve as the channel through which Southern Baptists "enable all persons in other countries around the world to hear the gospel of Jesus Christ as rapidly as possible, and, upon their response" to gather them in local churches.

The following comments reflect not only my own views, but also the views of a number of individuals with whom I have had conversations both within and without the organization. Though I will begin with the strengths of the program, each has its downside. This will be evident in the review of the weaknesses.

Obvious Strengths of the IMB Mission Program

Its history and worldwide involvement. Though not as old as some mission agencies, such as the Baptist Mission Society of London (1792) or the American Board of Commissioners for Foreign Missions (1810), now the Board of World Ministries of the United Church of Christ, the International Mission Board of the SBC has been functioning continuously for more than one hundred fifty years. Until after World War II its activities were limited to: China, Nigeria, Italy, Mexico, Brazil, Japan, Argentina, Macao, Uruguay, Chile, Israel, Romania, Spain, Hungary, and Yugoslavia.[2] The Board now has missionaries serving in more than 120 countries.

The long history and generations of experience. These are not inconsequential. Those who know the history of the FMB/IMB, however, are aware that the continuity that long characterized Southern Baptist foreign mission work has become primarily organizational. It now appears that since the early 1990s much of what the Board, its administrators, and missionaries had learned during the preceding century and a half frequently has been disregarded by trustees and other officers who willy-nilly changed policies, personnel, and direction.

The IMB is one of the largest missionary-sending agencies in the world. For Southern Baptists, long accustomed to measuring the worth of their efforts statistically, the IMB's numbers are significant. There are over 700 Protestant mission agencies in the United States. Most are quite small in terms of income and number of personnel, while as of May 1, 1997, the International Mission Board had 4,271 missionaries in 127 countries. The IMB, however, is not the largest missionary-sending agency in the U.S. Youth With a Mission (YWAM), for example, claims to have more than 13,000 missionaries on the field. However, the IMB can boast the highest number of career missionaries.[3] It is also the largest in terms of annual income. The top five agencies sending missionaries to other lands after the IMB and YWAM are Wycliff (2,300), New Tribes Mission (2,000), and Assemblies of God (1,500). The top five in terms of income are the IMB, World Vision, the Assemblies of God, Seventh-day Adventists, and Wycliff Bible Translators.

The support system—including a continual emphasis on prayer coupled with the most effective funding mechanism in history—enables missionaries to work with adequate funding and with minimal financial anxiety. They do not have to spend precious time writing letters to churches or individuals pleading for support. Their housing is provided, as well as transportation and medical care. Their income is above average for those in ministry. The cost of education for their children is paid by the Board, and this financial and emotional support continues for the children of missionaries even after they return to the United States for post-high school study.

The spiritual or prayerful undergirding, as well as much of the financial support, was for more than a hundred years generated primarily by the Woman's Missionary Union (WMU). Women in the local missionary societies utilized the mission study program prepared by the national WMU office, and prayer for the missionaries was once a major emphasis of WMU. Promoted at the local level together with the two annual mission offerings, the WMU was the principal sustainer of the FMB. The IMB now has a staff director organizing and promoting prayer from the Richmond headquarters.

The Cooperative Program—the SBC's primary funding mechanism—enables all churches, even the smallest, to be a part of a worldwide effort. The Cooperative Program began in 1925 and has grown steadily since. It is widely regarded as the best overall means of financing ever devised by a single denomination. It has some limitations and drawbacks, but all in all, no other Christian denomination has devised a more effective way to support its institutions and work.

The Lottie Moon and Annie Armstrong annual mission offerings both have wide "name recognition" and assure the two mission boards of millions of dollars each year above the amount provided by the Cooperative Program. For example, the IMB will have a total budget for 1999 exceeding $200 million, including an additional $100 million from the Lottie Moon Christmas Offering. Moreover, the IMB has sufficient reserve funds to meet almost any emergency or temporary downturn in giving.

The IMB continues to utilize people with a wide variety of gifts and experiences both as vocational and short-term missionaries. Missionary service has not been nor is it now limited to preachers, teachers, and medical personnel. Missionary service is not limited to college and seminary graduates or to the ordained. In 1997 in addition to the 4,200 plus career missionaries the Board supported, the IMB reports to have sent out 15,917 volunteers on assignments of a few days or weeks to several months. The Board still has a significant number of vocational missionaries working in jobs other than those of pastors or evangelists, but their work is increasingly measured by the number of converts and churches started.

A close connection has existed between the local SBC congregation, its mission emphases and organizations, together with other SBC training institutions. The SBC is composed of a network of entities, including the Sunday schools and other church organizations, associational, state, and convention agencies such as the denomination's colleges, seminaries, camps, and assemblies, which together continue to create a mission ethos or environment. Southern Baptists are conditioned from childhood to be aware of, support, and be involved in various mission endeavors. In this sense Southern Baptists have developed a "mission/spiritual formation system" par excellence, resulting in a missionary outlook or mindset that influences Southern Baptists individually and collectively, even those who profess no distinctive call to be a missionary. This mission milieu continues to exert a discernible influence on Southern Baptists. Thus, considering becoming a missionary is a natural stage or passage through which many, if not most Southern Baptist children, adolescents, and young adults pass.

Many hundreds of thousands of people in other lands have become professing Christians during these past 150-plus years through the work of Southern Baptist missionaries, and tens of thousands of churches have been planted. Moreover, besides churches a large number of other Christian institutions have been founded—such as primary and secondary schools, colleges and universities, seminaries, hospitals, and agricultural centers. I have visited more than fifty countries where Southern Baptists have missionaries. In virtually every case, Southern Baptist missionaries were regarded as competent, dedicated, and effective in their work. Their contributions, therefore, cannot and should not be minimized. Also, the institutions they established and maintained were highly regarded for the quality of their personnel and for the social, educational, and spiritual ministries they rendered.

FMB/IMB missionaries are well cared for, and until recently they had adequate material resources to do their work. As already suggested, Southern Baptist missionaries are among the best supported in the world. Unfortunately, maintaining that level of financial support has required major readjustments in budgeting. When my wife and I became missionaries in 1963—and for the whole period of the thirteen years we served with the FMB—the money provided for each country's work was divided equally: one-third for support of the missionary personnel, one-third for support of the national work, and one-third for capital needs (houses, automobiles, church buildings, camps, land, etc.). This apportionment has changed radically in the past thirty years. Today the lion's share of mission money is used to send and maintain missionary personnel. This is not necessarily an unfortunate development because it has removed one barrier to healthy relationships between missionaries and nationals over the matter of subsidy, that is, deciding which national programs, churches, and individuals receive Mission Board money. On the other hand, this has been one of the major reasons for the Board's ceasing to support institutions such as schools and hospitals. It is now clear that the top priority of the IMB is sending and supporting their missionaries, and the Board has little money to do anything else. Given the kind of world in which we now live, the question arises, should sending people from this country to other lands be the uppermost priority in light of what it costs to do this? Would it be a wiser investment to send a limited number from this country to supplement what the Nigerians, for example, can do better and more economically than North Americans?

Traditionally Southern Baptist missions were holistic in philosophy and in implementation. For generations the Southern Baptist foreign mission approach was proclaiming the gospel, starting churches, and meeting human need. It would, therefore, be incorrect to think of the work as limited only to evangelism and church planting. For at least ten years, however, the Board has steadily moved to focus more on evangelism and church growth and less on educational, medical, and agricultural missions. The institutions Southern Baptist missionaries established have not all been abandoned, but the subsidies once generously provided have been eliminated or curtailed drastically. Board spokespersons explain this curtailment by insisting that the institutions were established with the intent that they would become self-supporting. It would appear, nonetheless, that the principal aim of the IMB is to "win people to Christ," not to meet the wider range of human need through Christian educational, social, and medical institutions.

Besides winning people to the Christian faith and establishing churches, a large number of extraordinarily capable national Baptist leaders have been developed in the countries where Southern Baptist missionaries have worked. In every country where I have observed Baptist work closely, I have been impressed by the quality of the national leadership. Occasionally these nationals are featured in IMB publications, but few of them are known by Southern Baptist pastors and leaders.

The IMB's vast array of publications, including The Commission *magazine, are attractive and of high quality, and they keep foreign missions before Southern Baptists continually.* The published materials are among the highest quality provided by any denomination or mission-sending agency in the United States. The articles are skillfully written, and the photography in *The Commission*, for example, has won several awards for its professional quality. Anyone who reads this material regularly is informed about missions.

The growing number of FMB/IMB retired and resigned missionaries now living in the United States support the Board and represent its work in the churches, associations, and state conventions. This group of missionaries and former missionaries acts as effective public relations agents for the IMB, and despite any personal misgivings about what has happened in the SBC or at the IMB, they are consistently positive in their public attitudes and statements regarding SBC mission work.

The IMB has the infrastructure and the personnel to respond to natural disasters and other sudden crises in many parts of the world. The recent hurricane in Central America is a striking example of this ability. The IMB not only has the contacts with numerous organizations that do relief work, but IMB missionary personnel in Honduras, Nicaragua, El Salvador, and Guatemala are on site to work with and oversee the help Southern Baptists can provide.

Some Apparent Weaknesses of IMB Mission Work

Most of these weaknesses represent the "down side" of a strength. Some observers, of course, will not necessarily regard all of these as weaknesses.

The size of the IMB and its program coupled with the steady momentum and income provided by the funding mechanism separate individual missionaries from SBC churches. As a result, the missionary's sense of connection with and responsibility to those churches diminishes. While on furlough missionaries speak in many churches, but most Southern Baptists know very few if any of their missionaries. Most never see a missionary, much less have the opportunity to talk with one at length.

On one hand, it is good that SBC/IMB missionaries do not have to spend time and energy writing letters asking for financial support. On the other hand, they feel much more dependent on and have a much closer connection to the Board in Richmond than to their congregations. In terms of their financial support, most Southern Baptist missionaries feel little dependence on the churches. This is quite a contrast to Hudson Taylor's plan for funding the China Inland Mission.[4]

The Cooperative Program and the annual Lottie Moon Christmas Offering finance most of the IMB's work. These are incredibly effective, but are by nature and size impersonal. Missionaries are encouraged by the IMB in Richmond to promote both the CP and the Lottie Moon offering, but in most cases a missionary's promotion involves no more than an annual letter to family and friends with a paragraph describing the importance of these sources of revenue.

The way the Convention is organized, the IMB—as are all the other SBC agencies—is totally vulnerable to the group that has control of the Convention machinery. The controlling bodies that make up the Convention's boards and committees can be determined by the person elected president. In this sense, the president of the SBC functions more like the Pope or a bishop than the presiding officer of a democratic or congregational body. Also the SBC has virtually no checks or balances on its president's power. In terms of control and effecting change, the president of the SBC can exercise more control over the denomination's future than a president of the United States can determine the course of the nation's history. For the President of the United States must contend with the Congress, the Supreme Court, and the media, as well as with the people. And though the executive branch of government certainly wields enormous power, its power is counterbalanced by that of Congress and the Supreme Court.

The president of the SBC appoints the Convention's Committee on Committees. The principle responsibility of the Committee on Committees is to nominate the members of the Committee on Boards (now called the Committee on Nominations). The Committee on Boards/Nominations then "recommends" to the Convention in session the names of persons to serve on the SBC Executive Committee, and also the names of all the "directors/trustees" of committees, boards, and institutions owned and operated by the Convention. In 1979 the SBC was convulsed in a partisan struggle as the fundamentalist majority, by virtue of electing the president and controlling the two aforementioned committees, soon gained control of all the boards and agencies of the SBC. The character of the Convention along with the governing boards of its agencies and institutions was decided therefore by the group that won the majority vote at the denomination's annual meetings. Outside those meetings, there was no legislative body or court to which a minority, its number notwithstanding, could appeal for justice, nor was there any check or balance on the power of the Convention's president. This remains the case.

Support of the mission programs in the SBC is based more on patterns of behavior and emotional attachment to the organization than on accurate, up-to-date knowledge and conviction. If you were asked ten basic questions to test your knowledge of the history and work of the International Mission Board, could you pass the test?

Ten Questions about the International Board of Missions

Circle the correct answer(s).

(1) The first missionaries sent by the FMB went to: (a) China; (b) Nigeria; (c) Brazil; (d) India.

(2) In 1927 the FMB was confronted by a major crisis due to the: (a) Boxer Rebellion in China; (b) Embezzlement by the Board's treasurer; (c) Collapse of the stock market and the ensuing economic depression; (d) Resignation of Annie Armstrong as head of WMU.

(3) Who is the current president of the International Mission Board? (a) R. Keith Parks; (b) Jerry Rankin; (c) Adrian Rogers; (d) Robert Reccord.

(4) Which of the following is a requirement for becoming a career IMB missionary? (a) Unmarried; (b) Married with children; (c) Seminary graduate; (d) Under 45 years of age.

(5) What percentage of the Board's income is spent on administration? About (a) 7%; (b) 10%; (c) 13%; (d) 18%.

(6) The country where the IMB does not have any missionaries currently is: (a) Canada; (b) Mexico; (c) Russia; (d) Bahrain.

(7) According to its policy, which of the following would not be considered for appointment as a missionary by the IMB? (a) A person who has been a Southern Baptist less than five years; (b) A woman who has been ordained; (c) A pastor who has had less than three years experience; (d) A man or woman who has been divorced; (e) A woman who has had an abortion; (f) A person who does not affirm the Bible as inerrant.

(8) What percentage of the IMB's budget comes from the Cooperative Program? (a) 60%; (b) 50%; (c) 45%; (d) 35%.

(9) The management model used by the FMB/IMB is a (a) Corporate model; (b) Partnership model; (c) Team model; (d) Consensus model.

(10) Which of the following ecumenical relationships has the FMB maintained in the past? (a) World Council of Churches; (b) International Missionary Council; (c) Virginia Council of Churches; (d) China Christian Council.[5]

Because of its size and history, the IMB does not encourage innovation among its missionaries, nor does it reward boldness and daring. Moreover, the larger it grows, the more top-heavy it becomes with administrators and other functionaries. Institutions develop their own bureaucracies, and the larger the bureaucracy, the less innovation and risk-taking are encouraged. Institutions are inclined to reward those who "do their job" without making waves. The IMB, like most huge institutions, tends to discourage mavericks and reward conformists. Missionaries, however, have or develop skills that enable them to "bend policies."

Recently the IMB went through a major restructuring—ostensibly to streamline and lessen the bureaucratic overlay. Many within the organization questioned the need and the expenditure, but said nothing publicly. Few Southern Baptists, therefore, knew about the $6.4 million spent in refurbishing the Richmond headquarters, and one can only wonder whether the so-called restructuring will result in less or more bureaucracy. Moreover, will the spending of the $6.4 million in refurbishing the offices on Monument Avenue in Richmond produce any tangible improvement in the Board's work?[6]

The enormous income of the FMB has created innumerable problems for its missionaries and has made it difficult if not impossible for them to be the kind of leaven and salt that missionaries and all disciples of Jesus are meant to be. Having too much money is a greater problem for Christian missionaries than not having enough money to do what they are called to do. For many years—at least from the early 1950s to the 1980s—the FMB/IMB had too much money. Any mission program has too much money when it is unable to plan wisely and use available funds responsibly. Those who know the history of the FMB's work know that missionaries have not always been able to utilize the funds available to them in responsible ways.

Though the IMB is not awash with money today, in a world anguishing in poverty, affluence is probably the number one issue facing missionaries from Europe and North America. How can one justify living as an affluent North American or European, for example, in Bangladesh, Tanzania, Bolivia, or Haiti? It cannot be justified theologically or strategically. The problem, however, is not best solved by Christians in the West spending more on ourselves and our churches, reducing our offerings, or ceasing to give altogether. The problem can only be solved by a change in theology and by a radical change in lifestyle not only by missionaries, but also by concerned Christians and churches in the West who provide the funds for doing mission work in other lands.

For the past fifty years the FMB/IMB and its missionaries have tended to over-subsidize the work. Board funds have been used to build church buildings and other institutional buildings such as schools and hospitals for nationals; pay or subsidize their pastors and other church workers; finance their conventions and their programs; etc. I am not suggesting that this was unwise in every case, nor am I implying that the intended outcomes of subsidizing the work in Colombia, Argentina, Kenya, or the Philippines were bad. Overly subsidizing mission work for extended periods, however, without exception creates an unhealthy relationship, namely a relationship of dependency. Money in our world equals power, and those who control the money have and wield the power. But money, like power, can corrupt both the giver and the one to whom it is given. We have seen far too much of this in mission work. One positive result can be seen in recent financial developments. Because so much money is now required to recruit, prepare, send, and maintain missionaries overseas, less is available for subsidizing national churches, conventions, and their institutions. Thus, the age-old tension over who gets subsidy and who does not is no longer a major issue. In the meantime, however, many of the national conventions, especially institutions such as schools and hospitals, are struggling to survive. Some have moved to extricate themselves from FMB/IMB control.

Officially, FMB/IMB policy is to establish independent, self-governing congregations, associations, and conventions. In some countries, such as Nigeria, Brazil, and Japan, the national conventions and churches enjoy a great deal of autonomy. Having said this, it must be added that the FMB/IMB has never moved intentionally to integrate fully its missionaries and their work with the national churches or conventions. To achieve this kind of integration in the best of circumstances is difficult. It is impossible when the Board continues to work through what is known as the "Mission," that is, the organization composed exclusively of the missionaries in the countries where they have a permanent missionary presence. The time has long since passed when the Mission should have disappeared or been absorbed into the respective national Baptist entities, such as the Baptist conventions of Peru, Malawi, and Indonesia.

The first known Protestant missionary, Bartholomew Ziegenbalg, said in the early 1700s that ideally missionaries should place the responsibility for the work in the hands of the national churches and national leaders as quickly as possible. I have never known a FMB/IMB missionary who did not say this was the goal and the right thing to do. The familiar missionary litany goes like this: "Yes, the responsibility for the work here should be in the hands of the nationals. We want to do this. We will do it some day. But now is not the time. They just aren't ready for this much responsibility." In this regard the record of FMB/IMB missionaries leaves much to be desired. The IMB, as do the CBF and the Alliance of Baptists, talks a lot about "partnerships," but partnership does not necessarily mean the same thing to missionaries as it means to nationals.[7]

Reflect for a few moments and describe your vision of a true mission partnership:

- Between your church and a congregation in Honduras.

____

____

____

- Between your state convention and the Kenya Baptist Convention.

____

____

____

- Between the IMB and the Brazilian Foreign Mission Board.

____

____

____

The FMB/IMB is not and has not been since the early 1980s a missionary agency for all Southern Baptists. Early in 1982 and 1983 I first became aware that the FMB had changed a basic requirement for missionary appointment: Missionary applicants were required to study the doctrinal statement known as *The Baptist Faith and Message* and to write a personal response. Prospective missionaries were told to respond specifically and note any part with which they disagreed. If the prospective missionary did not affirm unquestioningly all of *The Baptist Faith and Message*, the chances of appointment were jeopardized.

How was this different from the way it had been? Prior to the 1980s prospective missionaries were asked to write *their own doctrinal statements.* If they were unsure or if they asked what should be included, they were pointed to a number of historic Baptist confessions—no two of which can be reconciled in every respect. The candidates were given a great deal of latitude. Once the FMB made *The Baptist Faith and Message* the doctrinal norm, however, candidates who questioned any part of the statement were subjected to intense scrutiny and prolonged interrogation. Some, of course, never got that far. Either they were discouraged from applying or they were advised by FMB personnel representatives to withdraw their applications. A few who had already been appointed were subsequently terminated for doctrinal reasons.

Today anyone who cannot or will not subscribe to the doctrinal positions of the SBC leaders and their theological and social fundamentalism need not apply for missionary appointment. The IMB, like all Southern Baptist Convention institutions and agencies, has become an institution bound to what amounts to a creed. Ordained women are not considered for appointment by the IMB, and married women with children who are appointed are designated as "church and home outreach" missionaries. Women who are specialists, medical or educational personnel, for example, are the only exceptions. Finally, the IMB is much more open to applicants who used to be called "independent Baptists" than to Baptists who really think and act independently.

One of the historical ironies of the Board's history occurred in 1996 when the FMB/IMB became a member of the Evangelical Foreign Missions Association (EFMA). Prior to that time the Board, like the SBC, generally shunned ecumenical involvement.[8] Now the IMB meets and cooperates with any number of EFMA mission agencies. Cooperation between missionary agencies is, of course, to be applauded. An outsider can only wonder, though, how the IMB openly and proudly boasts of its close relationship with the EFMA and its members while labeling the Cooperative Baptist Fellowship an adversary. In fact, since 1996 the IMB has refused even to receive money through or from the CBF.

In the past three years I have heard from a number of non-Baptist missionaries that IMB and CBF missionaries in certain areas of the world get along quite well and in specific instances work together. If the CBF continues to call itself a part of the SBC, is it not incumbent to develop some rapport and working agreements between the two groups?

The IMB, like the other agencies, is under the influence, if not the control, of some of the most reactionary, right-wing ideologues in the Christian church today.

- They do not place the same value on a holistic approach to mission as the FMB did historically.

- They do not affirm women in ministry, and they refuse to consider the possibility that women are as gifted for pastoral or teaching ministries as men.

- They appear willing to work with any "conservative" or "fundamentalist" organization, such as Campus Crusade, but not with Methodists, Presbyterians, or even the CBF.

- They do not affirm the separation of church and state, nor do they value authentic religious freedom—two basic historic hallmarks of Baptists.

- The Bible is no longer a sufficient authority and guide. Nor is *The Baptist Faith and Message*, as traditionally understood, considered to be an adequate statement of beliefs. Rather, it is the Bible plus *The Baptist Faith and Message* as interpreted by the Peace Committee and then amended by the 1998 Convention in session. These are the doctrinal pillars that are now the standard for Southern Baptists.

Historically, mission policy (the methods used by missionaries) was made on the field, not in Richmond. A missionary or group of missionaries, therefore, enjoyed a great deal of autonomy in the planning and the doing of their work. Several years ago all this began to change. Today more and more of these decisions are made in Richmond.[9] As in other situations, it may be necessary at times to centralize some administrative matters, and doubtless this is more efficient and less cumbersome than democratic, decentralized decision-making. If the recent changes in policy-making by the IMB represent an attempt to be more effective, they may prove to be wise. Given the way the fundamentalists have functioned since 1979 when they began to gain control of the SBC, however, what is happening in Richmond now appears to be more a means of consolidating power in the hands of a few people than improving the effectiveness of the missionaries' work.

The IMB still measures the effectiveness of its work statistically. Read, for example, the reports of the IMB, such as its "Overseas Facts & Trends," and you will see quickly that statistical growth—the number of missionaries, baptisms, churches, etc.—is the main emphases of the Board. Statistics are important but not the only valid measures. For the discerning observer they can reveal negative trends. Are then the numbers of baptisms, new churches, missionaries, and the like the most appropriate measures?

Tension between older missionaries—that is, those who were appointed by the Board before 1979 and those appointed after that time, especially since 1985—has increased. Some older missionaries have resigned in frustration. More appear to have hung on until retirement. Many confess that it is exceedingly difficult to work harmoniously with people who come to the field with a fundamentalist mindset. On the other hand, some IMB missionaries insist they have not been affected by the changes in the SBC, the IMB, or the new missionaries coming to the field.[10]

The IMB, like a number of other evangelical mission organizations, is attempting to place missionaries in certain countries where the governments do not grant missionaries permission to enter, live, or work. This is a highly charged and debated issue by many involved in missions. Some defend it while others believe entering another country "under false pretenses," even if it is for the purpose of evangelization, is ethically and legally questionable. They also wonder how effective a Christian witness can be when the missionary or missionaries have to work clandestinely.

Though the publications of the IMB are impressive and among the best promotional material available from any agency, a strong tone of triumphalism still comes through. The underlying message is: If the world is going to be won to Jesus Christ, Southern Baptists are the ones who will do it. Most Southern Baptists are accustomed to this kind of rhetoric. How seriously they take it, however, is impossible to say. They may be surprised to learn that outside the South and Southwest, Southern Baptists are scarcely known except by a reputation which is not necessarily positive.

The fact is Southern Baptists, despite significant contributions by their mission endeavors, will not evangelize Nigeria, or Ecuador, or Indonesia. If the peoples of these countries are evangelized, it will be Nigerian, Ecuadorian, and Indonesian Christians—some of them Baptists—not North American or European missionaries who will make it happen. The best help any U.S. denomination, church, or mission agency can offer to Christians in another land is spiritual and financial support. Then when requested, send a *select* number of personnel for specific tasks and for a mutually agreed-upon period of time. Baptist missionary personnel sent to another land, therefore, should be invited by the national church of that country—assuming there is one—and they should work under the auspices of the national leaders. Herein lies one of the problems: IMB missionaries have shown little inclination to work *under* nationals, and only under certain conditions have they been willing to work with non-Baptist national organizations.

Theological aberrations evident in Southern Baptist mission work are troubling. Finally, I must say something about what appears to be a growing number of theological aberrations evident in some leaders of the IMB as well as among many of the missionaries. If you read IMB literature, especially *The Commission* magazine, you can hardly miss the increasing emphasis on "power evangelism" and mission activities popularly called "prayer walks."

Those who promote "power evangelism" see the world as a spiritual battleground between the forces of good and the forces of evil. Moreover, they claim that Christians are called upon "to challenge the powers of darkness in the name of Jesus" and to exorcise or free those persons and places under the sway of evil spirits. For reasons that are apparent to those familiar with the core of the gospel and historic Christian theology, Jesus by his death and resurrection liberated us from this kind of spiritual bondage, and we do not have to engage in a constant struggle with demonic powers as if the battle were yet to be decided. To assume otherwise is to flirt with the principal beliefs of spiritism, witchcraft, and sorcery.

"Prayer walks" were initiated by a group of charismatics in California about a decade ago. As has happened in other instances, certain Southern Baptist leaders seized the idea as a promotional tool for missions. "Prayer walks" involve getting a group together, traveling usually by air to some non-Christian land or place such as Calcutta or Bangkok, checking into a nice hotel, and then walking up and down the streets launching prayers of deliverance at any place—building, temple, mosque—or at groups of people the prayer walkers deem in need of salvation. The first group of Southern Baptists I knew who went on a "prayer walk" went to Vietnam. Approximately thirty people went at the cost of $2,700 per person. If the intent of such trips is to expose the travelers to the conditions in a country and to motivate them to pray sincerely and earnestly for the land and its people, then such an excursion may be justified. Nonetheless, it raises a number of troubling questions. Is God so localized, remote, or indifferent that only when we are praying on site our prayers are heard? Second, can this kind of expenditure—thousands of dollars in airfare, hotels, and collateral costs—be justified given what we know about communicating the gospel? Furthermore, could an equally effective educational and spiritual experience not be had by engaging in a serious study of Vietnam, Buddhism, and missions, and the money spent for a "prayer walk" given to support those working daily in Christ's name in Vietnam, India, or any other place?

In this century a Christian commune called *Shiloh* was established in the state of Maine by an attractive, charismatic, and persuasive young one-time Baptist preacher named Frank W. Sandford. His movement and Christian community, however, became as controversial as it was different. One of Sandford's most novel ideas for world evangelization—and he had many—was to buy a yacht, sail around the world, and "claim" each country they passed for Jesus Christ. His was not a "prayer walk" but a "prayer cruise."

Shirley Nelson in her book on the *Shiloh* community describes Sandford's scheme as follows:

> The voyage was not a missionary endeavor in any way conventionally understood. On this journey the personnel would not go ashore to distribute the Gospel or teach. The trip was archetypal, but real. This little band... sailed out "to subdue the world for Christ" by a tiny white presence against the horizon, in the way that Joshua had marched around Jericho. Standing off shore, they meant to "take" the world by prayer, for only by prayer could the "covering" which blinded the eyes of humanity be removed.[11]

Sandford, his wife and children, and a select group from *Shiloh* made the voyage. They prayed for and "claimed" for Christ every country they saw. Nothing exists, however, to indicate that the trip was anything more than a grand, albeit dangerous and costly journey. No one professed faith in Christ. Not a single new Christian congregation resulted. In fact, the voyage actually planted seeds of doubt and disillusionment among Sandford's followers that eventually led to the disintegration of the whole *Shiloh* project.

One would think, given more than a hundred and fifty years of mission experience, that someone at the IMB would see the increasing divergences from healthy theology and rise to protest the cavalier ignoring of what the centuries have taught us about missions.[12] Perhaps some have tried, but their voices have not been heard. Until someone has the courage to stand up and say publicly, "What in Christ's name are we doing?" nothing is likely to change. Unless this happens or until another fanciful idea displaces "power evangelism" and "prayer walks," we can only be dismayed and saddened by the steady erosion of common sense and the leaders' obliviousness to the lessons of history.

Notes

[1] The purpose for organizing a new convention was stated in Article II of the Convention's 1845 Constitution, namely, "to promote Foreign and Domestic Missions and other important objects connected with the Redeemer's Kingdom."

[2] The FMB sent missionaries to Liberia beginning in 1846, but withdrew them in 1871. Prior to 1948, Israel was known as Palestine.

[3] Theoretically, a career missionary is one appointed for life or an indefinite period of time. The average "career" as a missionary, however, is less than ten years.

[4] The China Inland Mission, the largest missionary-sending agency in the world at the beginning of this century, was truly a "faith" mission. Hudson Taylor, who began the organization in 1865 to evangelize the inland provinces of China, *never* asked any person or congregation for financial support, and he prohibited his missionaries from seeking money directly or indirectly. They were mandated to depend solely on God and make their needs known to God through prayer. The CIM is now known as the Overseas Missionary Fellowship. "Faith missions" have long since abandoned Hudson Taylor's idealism and his method of funding missionary work. Though they may not ask specifically for funds, their letters to individuals and churches as well as the steady stream of brochures and pamphlets from their agencies are laced with indirect appeals.

[5] Correct answers are: 1.a; 2.b; 3.b; 4.d; 5.c; 6.d; 7.b, d, & f; 8.c; 9.a; 10.b.

[6] Of the $6.4 million for this building renovation, $2.2 million came from reserve funds and the remaining $4.1 million from the general funds, that is, the Cooperative Program receipts.

[7] See Appendix B.

[8] There have been some exceptions. Board representatives have participated, usually without fanfare, in select ecumenical organizations, such as the International Missionary Council and the Foreign Missions Conference of North America. But on the whole these involvements have been rare.

[9] See Appendix B.

[10] See Appendix C.

[11] Shirley Neslon, *Fair, Clear, and Terrible. The Story of Shiloh, Maine* (Latham, NY: British American Publishing, 1989) 286.

[12] In a letter to me written January 18, 1999, a Southern Baptist missionary said, "Prayer walks are now a required element in each [mission] team's master plan. To speak out risks not only being silenced, but losing your job."

"Gidada, though blind, was one of the founders of the Bethel Reform Synod in Ethiopia. Toward the end of his life he became increasingly concerned about the people in his own country, and so in his later years he went on mission to some of these peoples. He went first to the Bandas to tell [them] of God's love. The Bandas were amazed. Nobody had ever come to them to tell them anything good. 'Does God love even us, the Bandas?' they asked.

"Then Gidada went to the Anuaks, and he ate the food that was offered. They could not believe what they were seeing, and they leaped to their feet and danced around Gidada, because no one had ever come to them who would eat their food.

"If the blind can walk to peoples whom he could not see and eat with the despised, is it possible for those who can see?"

—from Bruce Gannaway, *Mission: Commitment to God's Hopeful Vision* (1992).

Chapter 5

The Cooperative Baptist Fellowship—An Analysis of Its Program

According to the Cooperative Baptist Fellowship's published statement, the mission of the organization "is to network, empower, and mobilize Baptist Christians and churches for effective missions and ministry in the name of Christ."

The Cooperative Baptist Fellowship was organized in 1990-91 in reaction to the finalizing of control of the SBC by conservative and fundamentalist leaders. The CBF was not initially formed to be a missionary-sending body, but a mission program resulted from a proposal presented by a task force appointed by the first moderator, Daniel Vestal. The program became reality under the leadership of Keith Parks, who took early retirement after heading the Foreign Mission Board for more than a decade.

The Apparent Strengths of the Program

Because the CBF is new and its mission endeavor newer still, the strengths and weaknesses of what is being done in mission is much easier to assess than that of the IMB.

The CBF mission program began with a unified view of the world and the mission—a global perspective. The old or traditional division between home and foreign missions—a dichotomy that may have had some justification in the last century—does not make any sense today. Even the International Mission Board has dropped the term "foreign," but its designated responsibility is in areas of the world outside the United States.[1]

The Cooperative Baptist Fellowship combined its missionary efforts, and no organizational distinction is made between what is considered "foreign" and "home" missions. This cuts down on the need for a separate bureaucracy and separate offerings and all they entail.

The organization is much smaller, easier to administer, and evidences the vibrancy of something new and fresh. With newness there is freedom and excitement. Moreover, there are fewer layers of administration. The entire staff of the CBF mission office is less than a dozen people, a mere fraction of the numbers employed by the two mission boards of the SBC.[2]

The CBF is far more open to different kinds of Southern Baptists than is the IMB. Though there are doctrinal guidelines, they are neither "fundamentalist" in substance nor in tone. Most of the missionaries sent out by the CBF are conservative theologically, but apparently are unwilling to submit to the doctrinal rigidity that characterizes the SBC and IMB today. The CBF affirms women in ministry and ordained women in mission. Some have questioned this, but the overall record of the CBF confirms it. In a recent General Assembly in Houston (1998), women were featured in a number of roles including preaching. Furthermore, those who have experienced marriage failure are not automatically disqualified as missionary candidates as they are by the IMB.

Because the organization is smaller, innovations and changes are much easier to achieve. Some critics assert that the mission endeavor of the CBF is little more than a scaled-down version of the 1980s FMB program. There are to be sure many similarities, due in large part to the fact that Keith Parks was the president of the FMB until his resignation in 1992, subsequently becoming director of the mission work of the CBF. However, there are significant differences in the two organizations. There is a place for missionary entrepreneurs in the CBF's approach to mission, and because Parks has had a sympathetic and supportive missions committee—the Coordinating Council's Global Missions Ministry Group (GMMG)—he has been able to initiate changes more easily and implement them quicker.

The CBF says there is an openness in its mission program to a diversity of gifts, and this appears to be true. One thing is certain: their standards for appointment are less rigid. Present gifts, CBF representatives say, are more important than past mistakes. Persons divorced, older in age, and with larger families are given full consideration and some have been appointed.

CBF missionaries, it is said, function as a team. To what degree this is true I cannot say, but officially the CBF does not send out individual missionaries expecting them to work alone. They are expected to function on the field as self-managed work teams without the supervision of on-site administrators. Each team or group relates directly to the Atlanta office without a layer of field administrators as utilized by the IMB. High in its list of requisites for its missionaries are accountability and collegiality.

There is an evident openness to work with a number of groups and even "secund" or lend personnel to other mission organizations. Occasionally the FMB in the 1970s and '80s did this, but it was infrequent. According to some leaders in the CBF, it is willing to work with any "Great Commission" group. Daniel Vestal has recently urged the CBF to look beyond working only with "Great Commission Christians" and to consider working with Christians in general. If this happens, it will move the CBF in a more ecumenical and inclusive direction.

The CBF Budget and Global Missions

Anyone who is committed to the Christian mission in today's world will be impressed by the stewardship of the CBF. Of the organization's total annual budget of $14 million dollars, more than $9 million or 64 percent goes to missions. This amount includes the 1998-99 global mission offering of $5 million. Most of the $5 million anticipated in the annual mission offering is designated for work with various "neglected" or "hidden" people groups. A breakdown of the designations is as follows:

Afro-Asiatic Cluster: $495,000

For ministries among nomadic Arabs or Bedouin in the Middle East and North Africa, including support of CBF personnel assigned to a clinic specializing in care for persons suffering from tuberculosis.

Altaic Cluster: $123,000

For evangelization of ethnic groups speaking languages akin to Turkish living in Iran, Kazakstan, and other countries of the Middle East and Central Asia.

Austro-Asiatic Cluster: $193,000

For agricultural, medical, and evangelistic ministries in Thailand and Myanmar (Burma) among an ethnolinguistic refugee group known as the "Rock People."

Austronesian Cluster: $817,000

To support CBF personnel doing evangelistic work with various Sundic and Malay-speaking peoples in Indonesia, Malaysia, southern Thailand, and other areas of Southeast Asia.

Central East European Cluster: $374,000

For sending and maintaining CBF personnel serving as liaisons with local, regional, and continent-wide Baptist organizations and churches in Poland and other republics of the area including the Czech Republic.

Diac-Sino-Tibetan Cluster: $123,000

For doing Bible translation and other work among Chinese, Indochinese, and various hill peoples living in northern Thailand, Myanmar, and southwest China.

Indo-European Cluster: $867,000

For work among a wide range of ethnolinguistic groups including the Farsi-speaking people of Iran, Gypsies in a number of countries, Kurds, and Albanians. Also, some of the money given will help support a Bible school in Siberia.

North Caucasian Cluster: $62,000

For the provision of medical supplies and other humanitarian aid to the largely Muslim Chechen people who have been at war with the Russians for several years.

International Diplomats Cluster: $195,000

For establishing and maintaining relationships with the diplomatic representatives from the nations of the world who work at the United Nations in New York City, in Washington, DC, and in Brussels. The latter city is the home of the European Parliament and of NATO.

International Ministries Cluster: $511,000

For ministries among immigrants, refugees, and international students in Atlanta, Miami, Houston, Dearborn, Michigan, and southern California.

Urban Ministries Cluster: $480,000

For ministry to victims of AIDS, families in crisis, and the teaching of English to immigrants in Miami, New York City, St. Louis, Brussels, and New Orleans.

Support Network Cluster: $323,000

For the Adopt-a-People program that encourages and facilitates the linking of congregations with specific unreached people groups, and for providing ways and means for short-term volunteers to be involved in mission efforts.

New Churches Initiative: $120,000

For the partnership with Friends of New Churches organization that encourages the beginning of new CBF missions and churches.

New Missions Personnel: $158,000

Supports the recruitment and processing of new missionary personnel.

Pastoral Care for Missionaries: $10,000

Provides counseling for missionaries and their families who experience difficulties and crises.

Prayer Engagement: $150,000

Supports various prayer programs such as Prayer Vanguards, Partners in Prayer, and Prayer Associates. Enlists individuals, small groups, and congregations to commit themselves to an active ministry of prayer.

TOTAL: $5,000,000

Current Status of CBF Missions

According to CBF spokespersons, 116 career missionaries are now under appointment. Some 25 additional individuals are working as "short term" missionaries with contracts from one to 24 months with the possibility of extending their service an additional 12 months. Ten persons are working with the CBF as "envoys," that is, they are employed by other entities and are in effect bi-vocational missionaries. In 1997 the CBF sent out 3,500 volunteers. Though little is said about individuals doing missionary work in "restricted access areas," such as certain countries in Asia and in North Africa, a significant number is doing this. The majority of CBF missionaries are assigned to "World A," that is, to those areas of the world that have had little or no contact with the gospel and with the church.

Most missionaries are engaged in evangelism and church planting, although a smaller number serve as "strategy coordinators." The strategy coordinators serve as advocates in the worldwide church for their respective people groups; facilitate or serve as prayer catalysts for these groups; act as advisors in the production of media featuring their people groups; recruit "tent maker" missionaries who will divide their time between secular jobs and mission work; encourage work with emigrants, refugees, and students; and encourage church planting among these peoples. The tasks of these coordinators therefore include surveying the needs of various "people groups" and suggesting ways of communicating the gospel to them—which may include such tasks as Bible studies, Bible translation, or dubbing and showing the "Jesus" film.

In the United States the CBF supports missionaries who are working with AIDS victims, teaching English as a second language, and doing evangelistic and social ministries among minority groups.

The budget for the CBF mission program for 1998 is $9 million—certainly the major expenditure of the organization. Though the CBF holds several million dollars in an emergency Missions reserve fund, any significant downturn in the US economy directly affects its work both in the sending of missionaries and in the support of their work.

Some Troubling Weaknesses in the CBF Mission Program

Being a new organization, one can expect it to be beset with problems which older organizations do not encounter. It is my impression that people in the CBF churches do have a closer feeling with the CBF leaders, and they have seen and heard more CBF missionaries than has the average Southern Baptist. Despite this positive relationship, Keith Parks and the CBF mission program have not generated the appeal and widespread following that he enjoyed while at the Foreign Mission Board. In fact, there have been frequent questions about his leadership and the overall program he has developed, such as:

Are the differences between the FMB and CBF approaches clear to the rank and file of the CBF, as well as other Southern Baptists? Accusations are often heard, even from loyal supporters of the CBF, that the differences are more cosmetic than genuine. I believe this to be somewhat unfounded, but it is a perception that Parks has been unable to change.[3]

Why does the CBF remain tethered to the SBC? The reasons are many, not the least of which is that a decision to declare independence from the Convention would largely be a symbolic gesture and likely result in the loss of many churches and a great deal of support. Furthermore, it would ignite internal church battles that pastors want desperately to avoid.

There are also legal questions regarding property ownership. Many of the churches outside the southern states, for example, were begun under the auspices of the Home Mission Board, and written in their deeds are "reversion clauses." That means that if these congregations cease to cooperate with the Southern Baptist Convention, the property will revert to the HMB (now the North American Missions Board). Whether this has been tested and whether it would survive a court battle, it is impossible to say. No church, however, appears ready to challenge it.

As long as the CBF remains a part of the SBC, the long-term future of the organization is cloudy. Outsiders often say, "If the SBC is what you say it is, why do you remain a part of it?" Some observers believe that if the CBF does not become independent of the SBC, the time will come—for some it has come already—when the younger and less informed CBF members will ask aloud, "Why don't we get together with the SBC and work out our differences?" Some observers raise the question as to whether the CBF as an organization could actually withdraw from the SBC, in view of the fact that in Baptist polity only congregations are counted as "cooperating" members of the Convention.

Meanwhile, many moderate churches, pastors, and individuals continue to support the SBC financially, but they have no influence whatever in the Convention or its agencies, and many SBC spokespersons have voiced the opinion that it would be better if the CBF separated from the Convention altogether. A special committee named three years ago studied the question of organizing the CBF as a new convention and recommended against it, and there is no indication that the question will be revisited again soon.

Attending the associational, state, and national SBC meetings and continually voicing a strong protest about what has happened and is happening may be better. The trend, however, appears to be that most churches that support the CBF continue to support the SBC, thus helping to pay for what is happening while being powerless to affect it.

The CBF functions as a mission society, and it manifests most of the strengths and weaknesses of this kind of organization. This is not necessarily bad, but it is dramatically and substantively different from the way the SBC functioned during its 150-year history. Most Southern Baptists do not understand the difference between the societal method and a centralized convention method, and therefore those who support the CBF see it more as an alternative mission board, not as a missionary society.

The Cooperative Program meanwhile remains strong and vibrant and is still generating more than $100 million each year. The CBF and its related partners, however, are not recipients of any Cooperative Program money. They must raise their funds as independent entities. Also these entities, such as the new seminaries and divinity schools, depend heavily on the budget apportionments of the CBF, which has no financial relationship to the SBC or any other national body.

The level of funding of the CBF is significant, but it is neither unlimited nor is it clearly assured. The recent flattening of its income over the past two years, for example, forced the CBF to make severe cutbacks in funding many of its partners such as the seminaries, divinity schools, and Baptist houses of study. Some have raised questions openly about the continued increase in the mission budget while cutting back drastically in other areas. Because time has not allowed the CBF to establish precedent, the slightest deviations, especially in income, can shake the whole operation. Many of the churches that give to the CBF are doing so as a kind of protest, not because they are convinced that the CBF way of doing mission is better. The real hope for the CBF lies in one or two directions: (1) Organization of more CBF churches, and (2) breaking its ties with the SBC.

The CBF and its mission program are vulnerable to the attacks of SBC leaders. Many CBF supporters still read the denominational publications and are exposed to all the "wonderful victories" and successes of the SBC. Likewise, they feel the sting of repeated criticisms of the CBF. This has taken a toll and forced the CBF to engage in damage control more than once.

The CBF relationship with the WMU threatens the future of the national women's missionary organization. The SBC leadership has marginalized the national WMU, and it would likely kill the organization completely if possible, especially if the women continue to refuse to submit to SBC control. "All you have to do," they are told, "is work with us exclusively," meaning, not have any connection with the CBF or any other non-SBC approved agency.

In some respects the WMU has a broader financial base than some of the newer agencies that have arisen and has the freedom to "partner" with other groups besides the CBF. But it is unlikely to have again the influence and role in the SBC that it once enjoyed, even if it were to surrender to the domination of the SBC leaders. In the historic Protestant denominations in the U.S., namely Methodist, Presbyterian, Congregational, and Episcopal, once the women's missionary organizations were absorbed into the denominational bureaucracies, interest in missions diminished. It is unlikely that the fate of the WMU would be any different were it to accede to becoming an agency under SBC control.

A struggle is going on within the CBF regarding its overall mission. Apparently some want to concentrate almost exclusively on "World A," while others feel this is not a balanced approach. A recent publication indicated that 60 percent of all CBF missionaries are working with "World A" people, primarily in evangelism and church planting. According to some CBF spokespersons, however, church planting is not the main activity of CBF missionaries. Rather, they are engaged in facilitating various ministries already in place among unreached people groups. The CBF encourages medical and agricultural missions, partly because these are proven ways to gaining entry to World A peoples.

A missionary approach that the IMB has imitated recently is "Prayer Walks." Prayer walks involve recruiting a number of people, taking them to another country or another place such as India, Indonesia, or South Africa, and once there walking up and down the streets launching prayers against the powers of evil residing in such sites as Hindu temples, Buddhist shrines, and Muslim mosques. The CBF recently announced that it too would promote this kind of mission activity (*The Religious Herald* 171 [March 26, 1998]: 7).

Apart from the enormous expense this kind of endeavor entails, one has to wonder about the view of God and the work of the Holy Spirit that prayer walkers hold. Possibly "prayer walks" are simply another mission fad that will eventually pass. In the meantime, however, what is it modeling for our children and young people in terms of sound and healthy theology?

Notes

[1] Domestic missions are the responsibility of the North American Mission Board, previously known as the Home Mission Board. Its offices are in Alpharetta, Georgia, an Atlanta suburb. Recently the top management of the two boards met together in the NAMB's new offices in Alpharetta to discuss their tasks, and an agreement was signed laying the groundwork for "a closer relationship" in order that the two boards "might lead Southern Baptists to reach North America and the world for Jesus Christ."

[2] It could be argued that some of the CBF's missionaries serving in the US are performing staff functions, such as the coordinator for volunteers and the Adopt-a-People coordinator. Also, the Finance Office of the CBF provides the financial services for the global missions program, whereas the IMB has its own finance division. The ratio of CBF staff to personnel on the field is about 1-10. The IMB currently has 4,570 missionaries and 482 staff positions, also a ratio of about 1-10.

[3] Keith Parks retired in 1999 and Barbara and Gary Baldridge were named the Global Missions Coordinators. Likely they will chart a somewhat different course for the CBF mission program

"The recognition that mission is God's mission represents a crucial breakthrough in respect of the preceding centuries.... It is inconceivable that we could again revert to a narrow, ecclesiocentric view of mission."

"We do distinguish between hope for the ultimate and perfect on the one hand, and hope for the penultimate and approximate, on the other. We make this distinction under protest, with pain, and at the same time with realism. We know that our mission—like the church itself—belongs only to this age, not to the next. We perform this mission in hope.... But then we must define our mission—with due humility—as participation in the *missio Dei*—the mission of God."

—David J. Bosch, *Transforming Mission* (1991)

Chapter 6

The Alliance of Baptists and Mission—An Assessment

If one compares the way the Alliance does mission, what should be the standard by which it is measured? Should the Alliance's efforts be judged by what other groups or agencies are doing? If, for example, the basis for evaluation is numerical or statistical, then what the Alliance is doing appears insignificant compared with the International Mission Board (SBC) or the Cooperative Baptist Fellowship (CBF).

A better measure may be comparing the Alliance's involvement in mission to the way Jesus and Paul did mission.

The Alliance and Its Involvement In Mission

The Alliance was not begun as a missionary sending body or a "missions" agency. It was organized in 1987 to make a statement about what was felt to be the repudiation and loss of historic Baptist beliefs and values in the Southern Baptist Convention. The adoption of the Alliance Covenant that same year was one of the first actions taken by the movement's founders, and the Covenant represents the core principles around which the Alliance was formed.

Today many feel that the most significant step the organizers took was the writing and adoption of the Covenant. Recently some have expressed the view that the Covenant should be revised to address issues that have emerged since 1987. However, the consensus is that the Covenant should not be altered because it addressed a particular crisis in Baptist life. Instead, the Alliance should adopt a new mission statement to reflect a vision for the future.

The Alliance Covenant

"In a time when historic Baptist principles, freedoms, and traditions need a clear voice, and in our personal and corporate response to the call of God in Jesus Christ to be disciples and servants in the world, we commit ourselves to:

"... the freedom of the individual, led by God's Spirit within the family of faith, to read and interpret the Scriptures, relying on the historical understanding by the church and on the best methods of modern biblical study;

"... the freedom of the local church under the authority of Jesus Christ to shape its own life and mission, call its own leadership, and ordain whom it perceives as gifted for ministry, male or female;

"... the larger body of Jesus Christ, expressed in various Christian traditions, and to a cooperation with believers everywhere in giving full expression to the Gospel;

"... the servant role of leadership within the church, following the model of our Servant Lord, and to full partnership of all of God's people in mission and ministry;

"... theological education in congregations, colleges, and seminaries characterized by reverence for biblical authority and respect for open inquiry and responsible scholarship;

"... the proclamation of the Good News of Jesus Christ and the calling of God to all peoples to repentance and faith, reconciliation and hope, social and economic justice;

"... the principle of a free church in a free state and opposition to any effort either by church or state to use the other for its own purposes."

At the annual convocation, which met in Washington, DC, in March of 1998, the following statement was adopted:

To keep faith with our Covenant, we will

- *Make the worship of God primary in all our gatherings.*
- *Foster relationships within the Alliance and with other people of faith.*
- *Create places of refuge and renewal for those who are wounded or ignored by the church.*

- *Side with those who are poor.*
- *Pursue justice with and for those who are oppressed.*
- *Care for the earth.*
- *Work for peace.*
- *Honor wisdom and lifelong learning.*
- *Hold ourselves accountable for equity, collegiality, and diversity.*

Even though the Alliance was not formed initially as a mission organization, one of the major concerns in 1987 was the radical change in policies being implemented by the two Southern Baptist mission boards. For example, early in the 1980s the Foreign Mission Board began requiring all who applied for appointment to affirm their agreement with the doctrinal statement called *The Baptist Faith and Message.* Prior to that time candidates were asked to write their own personal beliefs. The imposition of *The Baptist Faith and Message* was the first step toward assuring doctrinal conformity. Then in 1986 the Home Mission Board declared that it would no longer provide financial assistance to any congregation that called a woman as pastor.

The implications of these changes were apparent, and soon after the Alliance was organized, requests for financial assistance began to come to the board of directors from congregations and individuals. The only funds the Alliance had at that time, however, were from membership fees, and thus it was limited in what it could do. Word spread, however, about the multiple needs and opportunities, and unsolicited offerings began to come to the Alliance office. A Missions Committee was thus named to evaluate the requests and recommend disbursement of the mission gifts.

The Organization of the Cooperative Baptist Fellowship in 1990-91

Though the reasons for the formation of the CBF were similar to those that had led to the organization of the Alliance of Baptists, there were certain differences. For example, the CBF soon made missions its stated reason for being. Many Alliance people were involved in the organization of the CBF, and two were members of the Missions Task Force that prepared the original missions proposal adopted by the General Assembly of the CBF in 1991.

Initially it appeared that all the "moderate" groups would merge and become a single body. In the summer of 1992 an agreement was reached to choose a new name for the combined groups. All members of the Alliance, the CBF, Southern Baptist Women in Ministry, and Baptists

Committed would be invited to join the new body. For a number of reasons, not all of them apparent, this did not happen.

When it became clear that there would be no merger and no joint body, the Alliance offered the Cooperative Baptist Fellowship all of the Alliance's mission projects. The reason was to have a single mission program and avoid further confusion among grass-roots church members and division of moderate efforts in doing mission(s). A joint agreement was reached in September 1992. Two months later, however, the CBF elected Keith Parks as the head of the CBF mission program. The principles and approach approved by the General Assembly in 1991 were discarded, and a method more in keeping with the SBC program emerged. In a meeting with the leaders of the Alliance in Atlanta in January 1993, Keith Parks announced the CBF's willingness to include *some* Alliance mission projects in its missions budget.

After more negotiation, the CBF did accept several of the Alliance's mission projects, but not all of them. For example, the CBF declined to include in its budget the Fraternity of Baptist Churches of Cuba or the STRIVE program in the inner city of Chicago. Also not accepted were Baptist Peace Fellowship, Women in Ministry, and ministries to the homeless in Raleigh and Atlanta funded by the Alliance. These, the Alliance was told, did not fit the CBF's criteria of mission. The CBF would concentrate on evangelism and church planting, especially among designated "unreached people" groups. Thus, the Alliance faced an unfortunate dilemma. Either its partnerships with the Fraternity of Baptist Churches of Cuba and others had to be abandoned, or the Alliance had to continue its own modest mission program. The Alliance decided to continue to do mission.

The Alliance of Baptists Mission Statement

In promoting and supporting missions, the Alliance of Baptists will endorse projects that broaden and deepen the frontiers of God's reign on earth, and will attempt to build partnerships with people who not only embrace our Covenant principles, but who also are called by God to embody the gospel of Jesus Christ in their lives and in their work. The Alliance will particularly seek to assist new projects that take risks to reach the marginalized and forgotten people of our world. Finally, the Alliance will encourage the support of mission through the sacrificial giving of our talents and our lives.

What the Alliance is Now Doing in Mission

In 1994 the Missions Committee adopted guidelines that were affirmed by the Board of Directors. Prior to that time and since, certain basic principles have been followed. They are:

- The Alliance solicits funds only from congregations that have voted to support the Alliance principles and programs.
- In keeping with its Covenant, the Alliance provides grants without strings attached. The purpose of the financial aid is to enable, not to control.
- All requests are carefully investigated and none are granted routinely. Though some entities are helped for lengthy periods, all requests must be made annually, and they are evaluated to determine if they will be renewed or discontinued.

Mission Support Guidelines

The Missions Committee believes that nothing the Alliance does is more important than our global mission involvement. Moreover, the Committee believes that stewardship of the money given to the Global Mission Offering is a primary responsibility of the committee and the board of directors. Thus, the following criteria have been adopted to evaluate requests:

- *An expression of Covenant principles.* We should attempt to fund projects that embody some or all of the Covenant principles that define our vision.
- *Geographical diversity.* The Global Mission Offering should reflect some effort to be as geographically diverse as practical.
- *Encourage visionary risk-taking.* We want to support people and groups who dare to dream new dreams and imagine new and sometimes risky ministries.

- *The number of people being served in proportion to the amount of money invested.* This is an attempt to exercise good stewardship of the funds entrusted to the Alliance.

- *Honor connectedness.* The Alliance wishes to support persons and ministries that are of like mind and spirit with us.

Like other mission organizations, the Alliance's mission appropriations change each year. The following represent the distribution of the Global Mission Offering for 1998. These grants represent only a portion of a growing number of requests both foreign and domestic.

Non-U.S.A. Recipients in 1998

The Fraternity of Baptist Churches of Cuba, primarily to purchase property to start new churches, many being house churches already begun ($13,000).

The Baptist Theological Seminary of Zimbabwe, ($8,500) to pay a teacher's salary.

Kariobangi Baptist Youth Center, Nairobi, Kenya, to provide vocational training for youth and young adults ($4,000).

U.S.A. Recipients in 1998

The Baptist Peace Fellowship of NA ($7,500).

The Magdalene Project in Savannah, GA, a ministry of Union Mission to assist homeless women and children ($5,000).

Baptist Women in Ministry, a long-time partner, a program that provides support for women called to vocational ministry ($5,500).

Oakhurst Recovery Program, a ministry of the Oakhurst Baptist Church to minister to the homeless ($4,000).

STRIVE, an after-school tutorial program for children in Hyde Park Chicago district, an inner-city work growing out of the ministry of the Cornell Baptist Church ($3,000).

Center for Women, Inc., Richmond, for helping in the placement of women in various ministries ($3,000).

Northwest Corridor Chaplaincy program, Chicago, IL ($2,000).

Brite Divinity School Baptist Studies program ($2,500).

Emmaus House of Raleigh, an ecumenically-based ministry to homeless men. ($3,000).

Reconciliation, a Nashville, TN, prison-based ministry ($1,000).

Others

Cross Creek Community Church, Dayton, OH ($2,000).

Jefferson Street Baptist Community, Louisville, KY, ministry to the homeless ($3,500).

Dolores St. Baptist Church, San Francisco ($1,000).

San Leandro Baptist Church, San Leandro, CA ($3,000).

Providence Baptist Church, Little Rock ($3,000).

Note: Three of these churches have women pastors. All five churches are offering ministry in Christ's name in very difficult contexts and with imaginative, risk-taking approaches.

Evident Strengths of the Alliance Approach to Missions

- The Alliance became involved in missions in response to obvious needs and appeals. Though the amount of money given to the annual mission offering is modest, it has increased every year.

- The Alliance mission involvement is crucial to the continuation of many ministries, likewise crucial to the health of the Alliance itself.

- The Alliance has received and granted requests for help from entities who have been denied assistance by the SBC and the CBF, for example.

- In keeping with the Alliance Covenant, when giving a grant the Alliance demonstrates respect for the autonomy of the local congregation and confidence in the integrity of the recipient organization.

- Most of the entities the Alliance supports represent small efforts and limited constituencies. Also, several have been excluded from Baptist life or forced to the margins.

- None of the mission offering is spent for promotion or administration. This has proved to be mixed blessing. Regular promotion and administration of mission efforts doubtless would strengthen and enhance mission activity.

- All requests are carefully investigated and none are granted automatically. Each request must be resubmitted for evaluation every year.

- Decisions regarding use of grant money are made by individuals directly involved and responsible.

Apparent Weaknesses in the Alliance Mission Program

- Because of limited funds, the Alliance can offer assistance only to a small percentage of those who ask for help.

- Though mission involvement has been a significant part of the work of the Alliance from the beginning, the image of the Alliance is not that of a mission agency.

- In its attempt to do mission in non-traditional ways the Alliance has failed to generate the necessary awareness, excitement, and support. The true potential is not fully known outside the organization.

- The Alliance has not adequately publicized its mission efforts. Many individuals and churches that support the Alliance know little about its mission endeavors.

- Relatively few Alliance churches and pastors aggressively promote Alliance missions. Also a minimum amount of promotional material is available.

- Likewise, the Alliance needs in each church some group, similar to the WMU, to promote the mission offering and educate the church regarding the Alliance's mission program.

- Most congregations now associated with the Alliance must make a transition from thinking of missions in the traditional sense—thousands of vocational missionaries and millions of dollars—to thinking on a smaller scale. This transition may be difficult.

- Most requests received and granted by the Alliance are domestic. This, however, should change as the IMB and the CBF increasingly concentrate their personnel and funds on evangelism and starting new churches.

- A disproportionate amount of the Alliance's total income is used to maintain a very small structure.

Every recipient of the Alliance's mission offering is small and struggling, and represents a frontier of hope. Money and short-term personnel provided by the Alliance assists those who are working with people on the margins of society—people not seen by most of us, people easily forgotten or ignored. For them the Alliance is a reason to hope.

Part 3

Mission is not "a fringe activity" of a strongly established Church, a pious cause... attended to when the home fires [are] first brightly burning.... Missionary activity is not so much the work of the church as simply the Church at work.

—John Power, *Mission Theology Today* (1970)

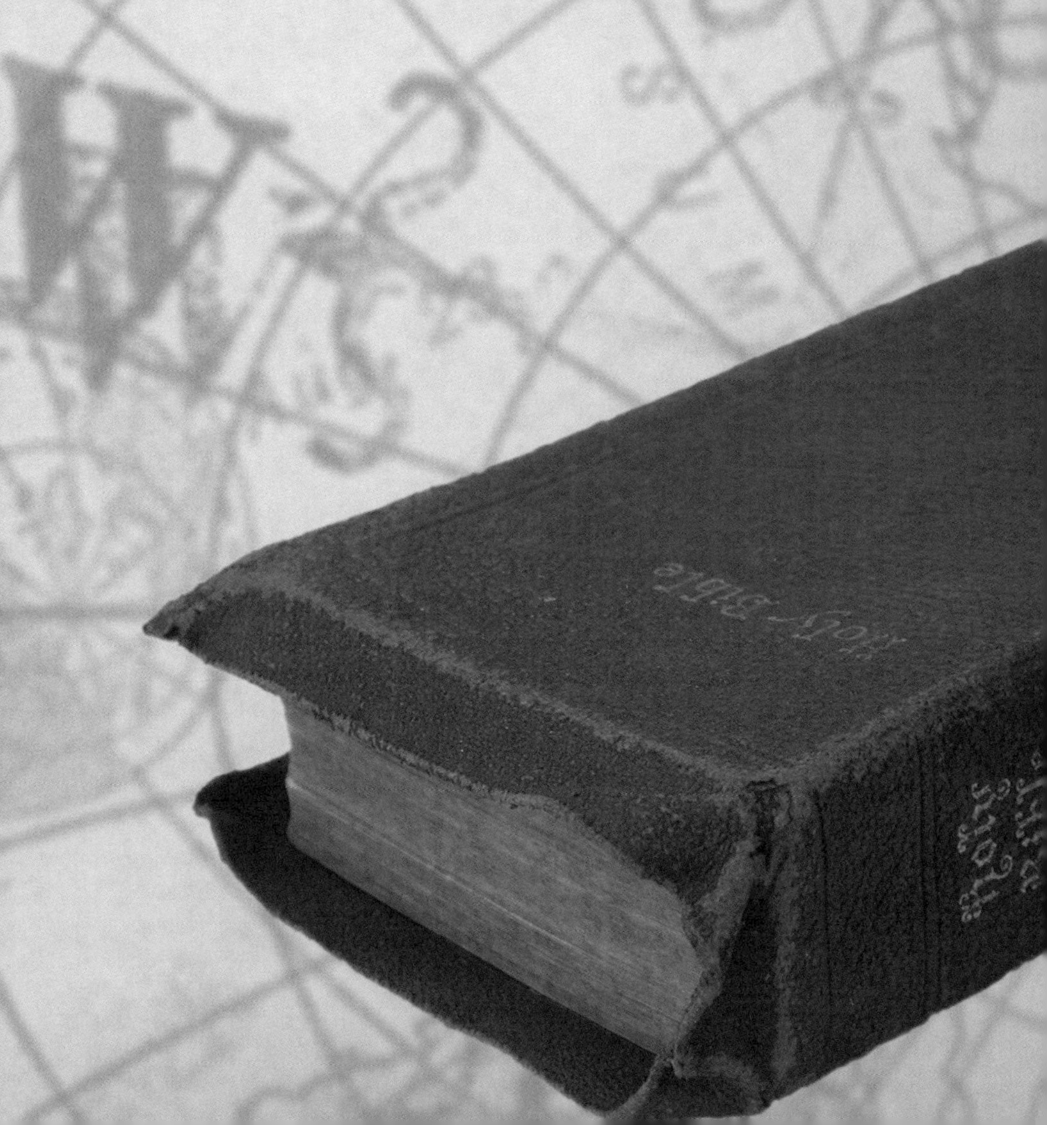

Chapter 7

When a Church Loses Its Mission, What Then?

The truth is, many churches have lost their sense of mission. This is the most daunting challenge the church faces at the dawn of the twenty-first century.

Recently I lead a four-day mission seminar in a large church. At the beginning of each session I invited participants either to raise their questions during the discussion periods or to write them on a piece of paper and give them to me prior to the next session. On Friday night I received a question I did not expect. The next morning when we met for brunch before the study session, I read the question aloud: "What do you do when a church loses its mission? Do you have specific suggestions?"

I could not help but wonder who had raised the question. Was it an oblique censure by a member who was displeased about what was happening or not happening in the church? Could the question have come from the pastor or some loyal member? Then it occurred to me that the question was being asked by many who are in a theological and programmatic quandary due to happennings in the world in general and particularly within the denomination. The truth is, many churches have lost their sense of mission.

I decided therefore to approach the matter by assuming the question was a sincere and serious inquiry, and that the questioner was not implying anything disparaging about his or her own congregation. So after reading the question aloud, I wrote on the board Emil Brunner's previously cited aphorism from his book *The Word and the World* (1931): A church exists by mission as a fire exists by burning.[1]

"What did Brunner mean?" I asked. What happens to a church that has lost its sense of and excitement for mission? Was Brunner implying that when there is no real sense of mission, there is really no church? A spirited discussion ensued.

Then together we developed the following strategy or suggestions:

Step 1

Be sure you are talking about the same thing, otherwise known as "working on the same page."

Our mission as Christians is to incarnate Christ in the world—say and do what Jesus did and respond to need as you believe Jesus would respond—and become a part of God's mission. This means that we need to discern where God is working and see how we can participate.

Our Church's Mission Statement

____

____

____

____

____

____

____

____

____

As you read and reflect on this statement, what do you understand it to say about the church's being a part of the mission of God?

Does it include communicating the gospel by word and by deed, accepting, caring, loving, forgiving, feeding, healing, teaching and...

Step 2

List the things your congregation is doing now to implement the mission described in the mission statement.

Our Church's Current Mission Involvement

Specific Activities

Budget Appropriations

Step 3

Gather basic information and reach preliminary understandings about needs and priorities.

Survey your community and list the needs that are most urgent as well as those that are chronic.

Local Needs

1 ____

____

2 ____

____

3 ____

____

4 ____

____

5 ____

____

(Use an additional sheet of paper if necessary.)

In Jesus' last meeting with his disciples, they asked him if he was going to restore the Kingdom to Israel. Jesus replied that this matter was in God's hands. Then he added, "But you will be filled with power when the Holy Spirit comes on you, and you will be witnesses for me in Jerusalem, in all Judea and Samaria, and to the ends of the earth" (Acts 1:8).

One of the changes recently evident in churches of all Christian denominations is the increasing tendency to concentrate more and more on local needs and devote energy, time, and money on themselves—new buildings, more staff, and more congregation-centered programs.

Is this true of your congregation? If so, do you think it is justified and healthy?

Step 4

Talk with knowledgeable people within and without your church.

A few phone calls to informed people can uncover areas of need you might otherwise overlook. After consulting with knowledgeable individuals, list needs in your town or city as well as in your state or geographical region. Place check marks by those you think may be needs you or your congregation should address.

Local Needs

1 ____

____

2 ____

____

3 ____

____

4 ____

____

5 ____

____

6 ____

____

7 ____

____

8 ____

____

9 ____

____

10 _______________________________________

(Use an additional sheet of paper if necessary.)

Look farther afield and ask, "What are some national and international opportunities for mission, and where can and where should your church be involved?"

National and International Opportunities for Mission

1 ____________________________________

2 ____________________________________

3 ____________________________________

4 ____________________________________

5 ____________________________________

6 ____________________________________

7 ____________________________________

8 ____________________________________

9 ____________________________________

10 ___________________________________

(Use an additional sheet of paper if necessary.)

Step 5

Recognize that there is no single way to do mission.

Every congregation has the responsibility as well as the opportunity to develop its own mission plan and decide the nature and extent of its mission involvement. Thus, a mission committee should:

- Begin by doing more praying—listening to God—than planning. Praying includes meditation, reflection, listening to each other, and critiquing.

- Know that the most acceptable, workable, and exciting ideas will come from within the congregation.

- Have confidence or faith that the necessary resources are available. This has always been true for those who are working according to God's will and plan. I believe the founder of the China Inland Mission, J. Hudson Taylor, was right when he said that God's work done in God's way would never lack God's supply.[2]

- Make the principal concern of a congregation "Are we following where God is leading us?" rather than "Where are we going to get the money and people to do this?"

Step 6

Avoid the most common mistakes.

The most common mistakes that mission committees make when developing a mission plan are:

(1) Rejecting ideas simply because they are new or unconventional.

(2) Assuming and attempting to do everything and meet every need. Ask yourself:

- What really needs to be done?
- What is being done?
- What are others doing?
- Where and how can we cooperate with them and support them?
- What is left to do?
- Whom is God calling to lead out in confronting a recognized need? Unless some specific person or persons step forward and say, "I believe God wants me or us to do this," the need, no matter how urgent, cannot be met.

(3) Institutionalizing too quickly what you are doing.

(4) Franchising or copyrighting good ideas or programs. If it works, share it willingly and freely with others.

Step 7

Develop a tentative plan.

As you begin to make some concrete plans about your church's mission involvement, be aware that there are three levels or types of mission:

- Direct personal involvement;

- Aiding, assisting, accompanying those you know and observe; and

- Enabling those you do not know, but who, after investigation, consultation, and prayer, you have come to trust and want to support.

The following are 25 examples of mission involvement. Write beside each the appropriate letter:

D—direct involvement;
A—aiding and accompanying those you know; or
E—enabling those you do not know.

___(1) You or other members of your church *tutor* inner-city children.

___(2) Send a financial contribution to Habitat for Humanity International in Americus, GA.

___(3) Be a member of a team that goes to Nicaragua to help in relief work.

___(4) Put $10 in the Salvation Army kettle during Christmas season.

___(5) Help in a "clothes closet" in your church or in another congregation.

___(6) Give clothes to a "clothes closet" in your church or in another church.

___(7) Be a member of a team that devises a means to evangelize an apartment complex nearby.

___(8) Work on a Habitat house in your town or city or in another city or country.

___(9) Make a gift of money or other goods to the City Rescue Mission.

___(10) Send monthly gifts through your church budget to the local Baptist association, state convention, or national body.

___(11) Work in a "soup kitchen" in your church or in another church.

___(12) Teach in an English as a Second Language (ESL) program in your church.

___(13) Support the proposal to open your church building to the homeless.

___(14) Give one night each month to help in a homeless shelter.

___(15) Be a member of a choir that goes to Argentina to sing and do Vacation Bible School work in the churches there.

___(16) Help to do a "census" or survey of the homeless people in your city.

___(17) Participate in a public prayer vigil for the homeless.

___(18) Write or call the members of the City Council to talk about the homeless in your city and what can be done to help them.

___(19) Be a member of the missions committee of your church.

___(20) Write an article for your church newsletter or giving a four-minute presentation in Sunday worship about your own mission involvement.

___(21) Cultivate friendship with a Muslim, Hindu, or Buddhist individual or family by (for example) inviting them to your home for dinner.

___(22) Assist an immigrant family to settle in your community.

___(23) Be an advocate for an undocumented worker who is being abused.

___(24) Repair and/or provide a car for a welfare mother who has a job offer, but no transportation.

___(25) Lobby the city council to provide public transportation for the poor.

Discuss your answers with others. Note similarities and differences. Develop a common list of activities and priorities.

Opportunities for Direct Mission Involvement

List ways that you as an individual can be involved, as well as ways children, youth groups, or adults in your church can be involved.

Ministry or Mission

____

____

____

People Involved

____

____

____

Budget Required

____

____

____

(Use an additional sheet of paper if necessary.)

Compare your ideas with those of others.

Opportunities for Assisting or Accompanying Others in Mission

List local mission efforts that from time to time may involve members of your congregation but generally represent efforts or programs of other groups or agencies, such as the city rescue mission. The "proposed contribution" is your recommendation to the church budget committee. Contributions may be monetary or "in kind."

Ministry or Mission

____

____

People Helped

____

____

Contribution

____

____

(Use an additional sheet of paper if necessary.)

Opportunities for Enabling Others in Mission

This last category includes being involved collegially or collaterally in the mission(s) being done by others, often internationally. Included are church budget contributions to the local Baptist association, the state Baptist convention, and national entities, such as the International Board of Missions (SBC), the Cooperative Baptist Fellowship, and/or the Alliance of Baptists. They would also include the annual mission offerings to these and similar entities.

Agency or Entity

____

____

Contribution

____

____

(Use an additional sheet of paper if necessary.)

Step 8

Review and evaluate the plan, making revisions when necessary.

Share your mission plan with the leaders and members of the congregation. Consult with respected and knowledgeable persons outside the church. Implement suggested changes that you believe will improve the plan.

Most organizations and agencies that ask your congregation for financial help know that becoming a "line item" in your budget increases their chances of receiving money year after year.

Review every mission item annually. If a program, agency, or organization no longer fulfills the purpose for which you initially gave support, consider investing your resources elsewhere.

Now the question: How do we implement the plan?

Ideas for Implementing the Plan

Notes

[1] Emil Brunner, *The Word and the World* (London: SCM Press, 1931).

[2] J. H. Kane, "J. Hudson Taylor," in *Mission Legacies* (Orbis, 1994) 202.

"The church exists in being sent and in building up itself for the sake of its mission."

—Karl Barth, *Church Dogmatics* (1956)

"The last quarter of a century of Christian thinking has contributed a great deal towards a fuller understanding of the nature of the Church.... In consequence we have come to accept in our generation that the Church of Christ is of God's design and not of man's making, the people of God, the community of forgiven sinners who have been entrusted with a mission. It is this mission which gives the Church its main reason to exist, to carry forward till the end of time the Mission of God."

—Paul Devanandan, *Christian Concern in Hinduism* (1961)

"The *missio Dei* institutes the *missiones ecclesiae.* The church changes from being the sender to being the one sent."

—David J. Bosch, *Transforming Mission* (1991)

Chapter 8

Making Mission Come Alive in Your Church

Nothing will energize a church more than seeing itself as part of God's mission in the world. The more people—members and adherents—who become involved, the more new life and commitment will be evident throughout the congregation.

Assuming the theme of mission is frequently emphasized in the preaching and teaching ministries of the church, the following are additional ways to get and keep the theme, the work, and the goal of mission before the congregation:

- Have a brief, clear mission statement that is regularly reflected on and, when necessary, revised by the mission committee.
- Inform the entire congregation of specific mission opportunities.

Mission Ministry Possibilities

Below are dozens of mission ideas. All of these have been implemented by one or more churches. They grew out of specific needs identified by a concerned member (or members) of the congregation. These center on local mission needs. Regional, national, and international opportunities would presume an additional list. Some require significant financial and institutional commitments. Others, however, cost little or nothing in terms of money. Certain of these also require a cadre of workers while others can be done by one or more committed individuals.

The following is not offered as an exhaustive list. It simply is a catalogue of some of the many possibilities for you and your church to consider.

For Children
Well Baby Clinic
Counseling
Tutoring
Programs for handicapped
Exercise and camping program
Daycare program

By Children
Be a friend to a lonely child
Help in doing work for elderly and needy
Accompany adult for "Meals on Wheels"
Help in a soup kitchen ministry
Accompany adult to visit elderly, nursing homes, etc.

For Adolescents
Counseling
Sex education program
Drug education & counseling
Friendship center
Tutoring
Reading center
Typewriting
Computer education
Drama center
Art instruction and display
English as a Second Language classes

By Adolescents
Tutor children
Provide yard work for elderly, ill, and disabled
Shop for elderly, etc.
Habitat for Humanity volunteer
Disaster relief team
Registration and form-filling
Surveys, such as, of the homeless
"Meals on Wheels" volunteer
Visiting/Sitting with elderly, sick

For Adults
Counseling for individuals and families: Abortion, Legal, Divorce, Funeral, Drug, Financial (debt restructuring)
"Meals on Wheels"
Assisting migrants and immigrants
Nursing home visitation and programs
Hospital visitation
Legal aid for needy
Medical clinic for the poor
ESL (English as a Second Language)
Provide repaired autos for jobseekers who are poor
Coffee House
Be advocates for poor (with city and state agencies), filling out forms, etc.

By Adults
Evangelizing–sharing the good news of the gospel to specified groups
Habitat for Humanity volunteer
Home repair for elderly and poor
Automobile repair for the poor
"Meals on Wheels" volunteer
Disaster Relief team volunteer
Visiting the sick, the elderly, and lonely
Develop and utilize skills to work with church drop-outs
Teach courses in dealing with conflict management, cooking & nutrition, purchasing, saving, and investing, job training, and ESL
Develop and use skills as advocates for the poor, migrants, and others

For Adults (continued)

Open the church to AA and other drug therapy groups
Courses on spirituality
Sitting Services for elderly, ill, and others
Employment and job training
Food Pantry
Clothes Closet
Ministries of friendship to groups such as college students, prisoners, military personnel, internationals, and homeless
Halfway House for released mental patients

By Adults (continued)

Attending and reporting to church on meetings of city council
Audio/video tape ministry volunteer
Be involved in inter-faith work
Food pantry
Be involved in peace activities (such as the N. A. Baptist Peace Fellowship)
Be involved in apartment ministry
Tutor school children and adolescents
Teach courses on spirituality

One of the most innovative churches in the United States, the Church of the Saviour in Washington, DC, has learned a lot about mission and ministry in its more than fifty years of existence. Almost from its beginning the congregation initiated a number of creative ministries, such as a Coffee House, a Health Clinic for the Poor, a housing rehab program for the poor, a ministry to abandoned and institutionalized children (FLOC, For the Love of Children), and a spiritual retreat center (Dayspring).

The members learned early that ministry to others had to come from the outflow and overflow of individual and collective spiritual life. For years they have had a program for spiritual development and a retreat center for learning to practice meditation, prayer, and reflection. Their commitment to spiritual development was the result of what Elizabeth O'Connor, one of the three founding members, so aptly described in her book, *Journey Inward, Journey Outward*: As one develops spiritually, there follows the vision and energy to engage in ministry to others.

The congregation has also learned that ideas for doing mission and ministry come easily. There is no end to what some think the congregation ought to be doing. However, it is necessary for someone to step forward and say, "God is calling me to do this." Once the need to address is agreed upon and someone is in place to begin and carry on the ministry, the congregation endorses it. Use the following suggestions to facilitate mission in your church.

- Provide times and means for people to inquire, investigate, and be involved in missions.

- Give those who are involved in mission—adults, young people, and children—opportunities to share what they are doing with the whole congregation. Many congregations set aside time in the morning worship service for three- to four-minute presentations which are regarded as integral to the congregational worship experience.

- Publicize in the church newsletter or other media what the church is doing and how every member can be involved.

- Develop a relationship with the religion editor of the local newspaper and inform him or her of the mission activities in the life of the church that are newsworthy.

- Name someone as minister of mission. Ideally, this will be a volunteer position. But in larger congregations, it may be wise of have a staff member with this assignment.

- Hands-on experience is much more appealing to most people. Thus give them opportunities to be involved directly. Doing mission will attract far more people than simply talking about mission.

- Ways to challenge a congregation and maintain a high level of interest and commitment vary. Learn what others are doing. If you are aware of a congregation that is known for its enthusiasm and its mission program, consult with the pastor and other leaders, and ask them for ideas and for any literature they use or publish.

- When you visit another congregation, try to find out what is happening in the church in mission. Bring back to your congregation information and materials that may be helpful to you. For example, the Ravensworth Baptist Church in Annandale, Virginia has for years published a "Mission Commitment Opportunities" booklet (8 pages). The booklet gives detailed information about the current ministries of the church. It lists specific ways any member, regardless of age or physical limitation, can participate. Also included is a commitment card on which an abbreviated list of mission opportunities is given. The reverse side of the card includes a commitment statement, the chosen way(s) a member can be involved, and space to sign one's name.

Ravensworth Baptist Church Opportunities for Mission

The following are some of the ways you can be involved in the mission work of this church:

___ Leewood Nursing Home
___ Working in "Clothes Closet"
___ Serving on Mission Committee
___ Visiting "shut-ins"
___ Praying for and/or writing missionaries
___ Cultivating people of other faiths
___ Working with homeless
___ Working with Habitat
___ Going on mission trip
___ Gifts to mission offerings
___ Serving on evangelizing team
___ Assisting (im)migrants
___Other: ____

Mission Commitment
Ravensworth Baptist Church
1998-99

Having acknowledged Christ as Lord, and having committed my life to him and to God's mission in the world, I commit myself during the next year to:

____

____

____

Signed ____________________________________

As a part of the congregation's annual stewardship emphasis, a Sunday early in the fall is designated as mission commitment day. All members are challenged to reflect, pray, and make a tangible commitment that Sunday by bringing their commitment cards and laying them on the altar.

- Publicize what is being done by members and groups in mission involvement in the church.

  The church of which I am a member regularly devotes four minutes in the Sunday morning worship service to hearing carefully crafted statements of individuals describing their vocational work and how they see what they are doing as a part of God's mission. It is called "Focus" time. These concise and intensely personal testimonies inform the congregation of the wide-ranging mission involvement of the members and effectively generates enthusiasm for mission commitment and engagement. Moreover, "Focus" elevates the daily work of the members to the level of Christian vocation.

  A sample letter to a "Focus" speaker is located on the following page.

These are merely examples of specific things various congregations are doing to raise awareness, engender interest and enthusiasm, and enlist people in the church's mission endeavor.

The question is, What remains to be done in order for you to implement your mission plan? Reflect on this and discuss it with others. Once you have consensus, begin the process of informing and inspiring the congregation to move to a new level of commitment and engagement in Christ's mission. This is your calling, as well as the church's.

Letter to Focus Speaker

Dear ____________,

Thank you for you willingness to present the focus during worship on Sunday, (Date). We trust that this time is still good for you. Knowing that it is impossible for you to tell your whole story in 4 minutes, we have developed some suggestions and guidelines that we think will help you as you make preparations for your presentation. Logistical information is also included.

Guidelines

(1) **Do** write precisely what you plan to say, and practice reading it aloud. Keep the written version in case you need to reference it during your presentation.

(2) **Do** be yourself and use humor if it fits.

(3) **Do** know that what excites you will excite others. Focus on an incident, crisis, concern, or joy that is important to you.

(4) **Do** relate how your faith connects with the questions and struggles you have experienced. State what support you need and where you find it. What keeps you going, and what is the best part of what you are doing? Make your focus personal. Remember, it is your story we want to hear.

(5) **Don't** talk about feeling unworthy, being nervous, or what you could have said had you more time.

(6) **Don't** rush. What you have to say is important, so speak slowly.

(7) **Practice** your presentation several times. Time yourself in the practice sessions to stay within four minutes. Otherwise, some in the congregation will think the focus is the sermon.

Meet the worship team in the sanctuary at 10:00 A.M. for final coordination. Together you will review the Order of Service, hear any last minute changes, and test your voice with the microphone.

Please leave a copy of your focus with your name on it in the church office for the archives.

Thank you for this significant contribution to our worship experience.

"The church is mission. That is to say, mission constitutes the ontological ground of its being.... That the church is mission means that the church lives for mission, subsists in mission, and derives her strength from mission. Mission is the heart of the church. The church is mission.... She is nothing but mission.... This means, and implies, a radical re-formation of the structure of the church in the light of missionary out-reach. This means the reconciliation of the world to God. The church which is not mission is not the church at all, in the true sense of that word."

—C. S. Song, "Whither Protestantism in Asia Today?" (1970).

Afterword

The Church and Christian Charity

"I was hungry and you gave me food. I was thirsty and you gave me water. I... was homeless and you invited me into your house. I was naked and you clothed me. I was in prison and you visited me."

"When did we do these things?" the righteous will ask.

"I tell you, whenever you did this for one of the least important of these brothers or sisters, you did it for me." (Mt 25:35-40)

We may think, mistakenly to be sure, that these words from Jesus' parable regarding the Last Judgment have been influential in the history of the Christian church only in modern times. A careful study will reveal that their impact is apparent very early. According to Adolf Harnack, these words "exerted so powerful an influence" in the early church that Christian preaching during the first three centuries can rightly be described as "the preaching of love and charity" (*The Mission and Expansion of Christianity in the First Three Centuries* 1 [1908] 147). The word "charity," of course, was a synonym for "love." Love for early Christians was much more than an emotional feeling. It can best be defined as love lived out, love exemplified.

Tertullian (d. 230), one of the Latin Church fathers, wrote for example that the churches of his era had a common fund to which members contributed monthly. Giving to the fund was not obligatory, he said, for no one was required to give. Rather, each contributed of his or her "own free will." Contributions to this common fund were, in Tertullian's words, "deposits of piety," and the money was spent to feed the hungry and bury the poor; it was spent in behalf of children who had "neither parents nor money," and in caring for the elderly who could no longer provide for themselves. The funds were also used to help victims of shipwreck and other calamities. It was spent to aid those who toiled in the mines, were exiled on islands, or languished in prison. The monies could be used for any of these purposes, as long as help to the recipients was "for the sake of God's fellowship."

In discussing this period of Christian history, Harnack elaborates on ten separate uses of the offerings given in the churches. The money, he says, went not only to support pastors, teachers, and other church officials. The money was also used to care for widows and orphans; the sick and the disabled; individuals in prison and those forced to work in the mines. Churches likewise assumed responsibilities for burying the dead (especially the poor) and for caring for slaves and victims of natural disasters. Likewise offerings were used to provide jobs for the unemployed, offer hospitality to Christian brothers and sisters who were traveling, and send relief to congregations suffering in poverty or other perils (pp. 153-181). These practices continued in succeeding centuries.

One of the curious aspects of the sixteenth-century Reformation and the Reformers, however, was that Martin Luther, John Calvin, and their colleagues, even though they rested their case on the Bible—especially on the New Testament—they did not preoccupy themselves with spreading the gospel to other lands. Several reasons are offered to explain their neglect, among them being that the Reformers seemingly believed that the mandate to carry the gospel to the uttermost parts of the earth had been fulfilled during the first century, that is, during the time of the Apostles.

Significant Protestant missionary involvement and missionary projects in foreign lands, therefore, did not begin until the seventeenth century when two young German Lutheran Pietists, Bartholomew Ziegenbalg and Henry Plütschau, were sent to India in 1705, nearly two centuries after the beginning of the Reformation. Plütschau did not remain long in India, and Ziegenbalg died in 1719. They developed, nonetheless, a missionary approach and established a pattern that was generally followed by their Protestant missionary successors until the twentieth century.

Ziegenbalg and Plütschau were sent to India with explicit instructions to give themselves to the preaching of the gospel—nothing more and nothing less. Their task as missionaries was, they were told, "the saving of individual souls." The two young missionaries, however, soon discovered that "saving souls" in another culture was not that simple, and they became increasingly involved not only in preaching, but also in education, Bible translation, social work, and medical care. When the Mission Secretary in Europe learned what Ziegenbalg and Plütschau were doing, he admonished them to limit themselves to preaching and to refrain from being involved in "earthly affairs." Ziegenbalg replied, saying in effect that their educational, social, and medical work were not a violation of their mandate nor an abandonment of their missionary task. Their holistic approach to mission stemmed rather from their concern for the personal salvation of the Indian people.[1]

Though there is no evidence that these two young missionaries appealed to the precedent established by their Lutheran forebears, they well could have. For the early Pietist leaders in Europe set an example by establishing hundreds of schools, hospitals, sanitariums, and other charitable institutions to educate children and youth and to help the sick and the needy.[2]

This approach to missions by Protestants, both domestic and foreign, was commonplace for more than two hundred years, and according to several well-known evangelical scholars, this inclusive or holistic approach to missions was the accepted way to do missionary work both for Protestants and Catholics until the early decades of the twentieth century. What prompted the change? The change, called the "great reversal" by one evangelical scholar, came as a result of an overreaction by many evangelicals and fundamentalists to the "social gospel" and to what they perceived to be theological liberalism. The result was a narrowing of the missionary task by evangelicals and fundamentalists to evangelism or "preaching the gospel" and to church planting. It was, says Roger Greenway, "a backlash against liberalism," and "the inheritors of the evangelical tradition went into a period of retreat and separatism which had a profound impact on their social concern. All progressive social concern was almost eliminated among evangelicals by the end of the 1900-1930 period," says Greenway.[3] Though I believe this is somewhat overstated, Greenway does have a point.

Until the 1980s, the Foreign Mission Board and the Home Mission Board of the Southern Baptist Convention, for example, did not follow the lead of the evangelicals and fundamentalists described by Greenway. Rather, until the 1980s the SBC boards encouraged a comprehensive approach to mission, and they supported a broad range of missionary activities—not only evangelism and church planting, but also educational, medical, agricultural, and social work. Only in the last two decades has the traditional Protestant mission philosophy been deemphasized and largely, though not entirely, replaced by the evangelical and fundamentalist approach. Mission leaders at the two SBC boards deny their social concerns have diminished. But their increasing tilt toward evangelism and church planting at the expense of a broader and more comprehensive approach is evident to anyone who is familiar with the current emphases in the SBC seminaries, the tasks assigned to new missionary appointees, the allocation of funds, and the publications of the two mission boards.

Ironically, at a time when many evangelicals were recognizing the mistake in separating evangelism and social concerns—nearly 75 years after the "great reversal"—the SBC began abandoning its holistic mission tradition in favor of more and more emphasis on evangelism and church planting.[4]

Many have made categorical pronouncements about what is required "to be saved." They quote the words of Simon Peter, the Apostle Paul, or their favorite evangelist. According to what Jesus said, the saved will be those who show charity for "the least" of those we encounter.

Notes

[1] See Stephen Neill, *A History of Christian Missions* (Penguin Books, 1986) 195-7. Though only 23 years old when he set out for India, Ziegenbalg developed a clear mission philosophy. According to Stephen Neill, five "principles stand out clearly from the beginning" of Ziegenbalg's work: (1) The church and the school could not be separated. Christians, he reasoned, should be able to read the Bible. (2) Consequently, the Bible had to be translated into their language, and Christian children and youth had to be educated. (3) If the gospel were to be understood by their Indian hearers, the missionaries needed to know the Indian culture and understand the way the people thought. (4) The ultimate goal was personal conversion and salvation, but concern for the "soul" required a concern for the whole person. (5) A church truly Indian with Indian leadership, Ziegenbalg contended, should be developed as quickly as possible.

[2] See Johannes Verkuyl, *Contemporary Missiology*, trans. by Dale Cooper (Grand Rapids MI: Eerdmans, 1978) 177.

[3] See Roger Greenway, *Together Again* (Monrovia CA: MARC, 1998) 15. Greenway is professor of missiology at Calvin Theological Seminary, Grand Rapids, Michigan.

[4] See Appendix E.

Appendixes

Appendix A

"Hands-on Missions"

Three couples were recently discussing their changing views of mission. "I just don't get excited any more about long-distance missions," one of them said. "What excites me are the needs and opportunities to do mission right here in our own city." Everyone in the room voiced agreement. Such comments are frequently heard. What made this declaration unusual was that the person who said it was once a career missionary who was talking to five other former missionaries.

In previous generations excitement about foreign missions was commonplace. It energized congregations to study, to pray, and to raise huge sums of money for "the missionaries." Today, however, that kind of ardor has dissipated noticeably in most mainline denominations and churches, and in its place there has developed a growing interest in and commitment to "hands-on" missions across the street or across the world. Mission boards and agencies continue aggressively to recruit individuals as career missionaries, but there is a steady and ever-enlarging stream of volunteers, individuals and congregations who want go to Europe, Asia, Africa, and Latin America as short-term missionaries. In a sense, they are "standing in line" and clamoring for places to go on "mission trips."

The experience of Charles and Wanda Hobson in Nogales, Arizona, is an indication of what is happening. After serving for more than fifteen years as FMB missionaries in Colombia, Paraguay, and Argentina, the Hobsons returned to the United States in the 1970s. Charles pastored a church in California and later one in Oregon. He "retired" in June 1997 and moved to Arizona. There he assumed the pastorate of the Nogales Baptist Church, a small, seven-year-old, bilingual congregation located near the U.S. border with Mexico, an ideal place for two people with the energy of the Hobsons who are fluent in English and Spanish.

Before moving to Arizona, Charles and Wanda decided they would begin their work in Nogales with two Vacation Bible Schools, one in English and the other in Spanish. They placed an announcement in the *Help Wanted... On Site* section of a Home Mission Board publication and soon began receiving calls from churches and individuals who indicated an interest in coming that summer to Nogales. Two of the churches who contacted the Hobsons were the First Baptist Church (English-speaking) and the First Hispanic Baptist Church of Carrollton, Texas. Not only did they offer to send workers, but they also indicated they would provide whatever supplies the Hobsons thought would be needed. The churches did what they promised, and they commissioned two teams of workers and filled two vans with supplies.

These first teams of short-term missioners were followed by additional volunteers from Oregon, Georgia, and Phoenix, Arizona. In fact, there was a steady stream of volunteers who came at their own expense to assist the Hobsons.

During the fall and winter of 1997-98 other individuals and groups called, saying they would like to come to Nogales. "We decided, therefore, to pull out all the stops and go all out," Hobson says. "We invited all we thought we could productively utilize." A group of women from Virginia arrived first. They were followed by a contingent of youth and adult sponsors from Savannah, Georgia. They helped conduct a VBS in Nogales and then an extension VBS in Rio Rico, a town just across the border. While in Mexico, the Georgia team became aware of the needs of an orphanage in Imuris—the *Orfanatorio Casa Elisabet* (Elizabeth House Orphanage), and after returning home they sent money to buy solar panels for the institution. Later, they went back to Mexico and spent a week installing doors, doing repair work, and upgrading the orphanage facilities. During the second week of that trip the Hobsons took the volunteers deep into Mexico for worship services and Bibles distribution. Currently this Savannah, Georgia, congregation is raising money to buy a garden tractor for the orphanage so that some of the food needed by the institution can be planted and harvested on site. Besides these mission groups, a congregation in Clovis, New Mexico, sent their youth to Nogales during spring break of 1998. They painted the town's rescue mission and did additional work for the orphanage in Imuris.

"Churches call regularly," says Hobson. "They all say the same thing. They want 'hands-on experience,' and they ask if we can use them. These are not churches that have reduced their financial support of the denomination. In fact, they assure us that they give faithfully to the annual mission offerings as well as support the denomination's Cooperative Program." What has changed, Hobson stresses, is that churches and members no longer are satisfied to give only their money. "They want to be involved personally, directly."

An article in *The Biblical Recorder* states the shift in the way mission is being done today is related to younger persons' experiences and outlook on life.[1] Most young people are unimpressed by "big programs and big solutions." They are not willing to depend on surrogates to do the work for them. They prefer to be involved, even if it is only by trying to help one or two people they can see. Giving money to an impersonal program or agency that claims to be "tackling the world" does not do much for them. Also this younger generation has the resources to go where they want to go, and they see the whole world as reachable. Unlike times past, every country in the world is reachable in a matter of hours by jet. And while traditionalists continue to debate whether mission should be evangelism or social ministry, younger people fail to see any dichotomy between the two. As the director of one inner-city volunteer mission program said recently, "If you're talking about Jesus while you're building a house, which are you doing?"

An episode of the popular sitcom *Dharma and Greg* mirrors the attitude of many young adults.

Dharma, a "free-spirited and idealistic daughter of 1960s hippies," learns that the young woman checking her groceries at the supermarket is pregnant, single, unprepared and unable to take care of a child.

The checkout woman's problem becomes Dharma's problem, and she resolutely promises to help the young mother. What better way than to offer to adopt the child once it has been born? The challenge, however, is to convince Greg, her husband, that this is the thing they should do.

Greg, however, is less than enthusiastic. In fact he is completely nonplused. Adopt a child of a woman who works at the supermarket? The idea is preposterous. Though Greg is not completely unsympathetic with the young pregnant woman's dilemma, he keeps trying to make Dharma see that there are people and "organizations set up to handle this kind of thing."

Dharma, nevertheless, is determined. Greg finally vents his frustration and feelings saying, "I'm sorry, Dharma, but you can't help every human being on the planet."

"Yeah, but Greg, you can help the ones that are right in front of you."[2]

That is precisely what people born in the 1960s and '70s want to do. If the church is not agreeable and responsive, they will find and do their mission in other places.

[1] Andrew Black, "Generation X Views Missions as Hands-on Proposition," *The Biblical Recorder* 165 (Jan 16, 1000):5.

[2] Ibid.

Appendix B

A Letter from Latin America

About a year ago I received a letter from well-known Latin American Baptist leader Manuel Gutierrez.* He was distressed and upset about the announced re-structuring of the Foreign Mission Board in Richmond. He wrote:

Dear Alan:

We have now to suffer a new aggression to our common bond in the Lord ("Bless be the tie that binds..."). Are some more "binded" than others? This new aggression has been executed by our brothers in the FMB/SBC. Now they are calling the Board the International Mission something or other. They have "rearranged" their field work according to a rationale that makes sense only in the mind of I do not know who. Not only will this complicate our common work in Latin America more than it has been till now, but they have done this without consulting with anybody here.

What do we have to do now? I know. We have to suffer in silence a new aggression. Brother, I am fed up. Either we work together or we work for them. I am not willing to work for people who do not consult about decisions that affect us. For this means that we are not brothers and sisters. It means they are the masters and we are the slaves.

But I have been freed by the Lord, and I am not willing to relinquish my freedom to any form of slavery. If we are working "together" for Christ, then we can work with anybody. But not this way. We are Baptists, and we do not have bishops or cardinals.

This is an example of what I was talking about recently in our meeting. Some people, I said, think the world belongs to them. They are the owners, and they can decide for others without any consultation.

Alan, I am sorry to bother you with my pain, and I hope you will understand my feelings.

Another problem is that we learned of this new "arrangement" in a very unofficial way—by means of the missionaries who are our friends, who came and informed us what they learned officially.

When they need us for any of their purposes, they come and ask for time on our programs, and they speak of our "partnership," and all that.... But when they want to make decisions—such as this re-organization that will affect our Baptist work in Latin America—they do not even bother to discuss it with us. Partnership seems to be something they talk about when they want something from us, but it is hardly a true partnership.

As a matter of personal respect—after being allowed to work in Latin America all these years (for this area of the world does not belong to Southern Baptists)—they at least should have the courtesy to discuss things with us.

I will be frank to say, my friend, that this sense of dismay is not only mine. It is a common feeling among many of us here, and it came out most recently in one of our meetings.

We have no way of manifesting our disagreement officially with these new policies, and I suspect that some will not say anything for fear of retaliation. But those of us here in Latin America feel very despised, disdained, disregarded, ignored, omitted, overlooked—that is, not important at all to you in North America. Oh, we are "important" when there is "dirty work" to be done. But when it comes to decisions that can affect our "common" work, our views are not sought at all.

When these kinds of things happen, Alan, I feel like "throwing in the towel" as far as working together is concerned. Let someone else try to work with people who never consult you about what they do—some poor stupid, moronic, obtuse guy who, for a few dollars, will be willing to forget his high calling to freedom and will be inclined to do whatever those in the FMB/SBC wish.

I hope my comments do not reach you at a bad time. I would hate to add to your burdens. On the other hand, you are the kind of friend to whom I can bare my soul.

Love and peace,
(Signed) Manuel

Name has been changed.

Appendix C

Southern Baptist Missions—A Case Study

James Becker*, professor of missions in North Central Baptist Seminary*, is troubled. Besides teaching his classes, he is often asked to speak on missions in churches and before church groups. Consequently, he continually tries to keep abreast of what is happening, not only in regard to the mission boards, but also in relation to what is happening with the missionaries. Lately he has been particularly troubled by changes in the SBC, especially those affecting the Foreign and Home Mission boards. The abrupt retirement of Keith Parks in 1992 and his subsequent acceptance of the position as director of the Cooperative Baptist Fellowship's mission program intensified Becker's anxiety. He wondered if more resignations would follow.

He therefore decided to write directly to several missionaries he had taught in seminary and ask for their assessments of what was happening. Most of them responded quickly and showed a willingness to discuss what was taking place, but they wanted their comments to be held in confidence. Becker was not surprised by what the missionaries said, but it was informative. The letter from Paul Smith, however, did greatly surprise Becker.

The Smiths, FMB Missionaries to Mas Al-Mar

Paul and Linda Smith* served as journeymen with the FMB before they married and enrolled in the seminary. Though fairly young, they were an impressive couple who made it known that they were planning to become career missionaries as soon as possible. Both took courses in missions, and they were good students.

Following graduation and the requisite church experience, they were appointed in the mid-1980s as missionaries to Mas Al-Mar. Because of their journeymen experience with the Foreign Mission Board and their occasional letters about their family and their work, Becker felt they would be the kind of individuals he could write and ask for their candid evaluation. He knew they were in the U.S. on furlough because they had written to him from Alabama. So in February he sent them an e-mail as follows:

*Names have been changed.

Dear Paul and Linda,

Before you finish your furlough and go back to the field, I hope we can see you. I appreciated receiving your Christmas letter and having the latest news about your family and your work.

This March and April I am to speak in two very fine churches. They want me to do mission studies. I am sure I will be asked questions about what has happened with our foreign mission board work, so would you help me by telling me what you think and feel about the mission program of the FMB and any feeling you may have about the CBF or the Alliance of Baptists. I want to be accurate and objective in what I say. As you well know, I do have a responsibility to the denomination, but I don't want to promote one of these at the expense of the others. Neither do I want to be unfair in criticizing any of them. In order to be accurate and objective, I need some help from people like you whom I respect and trust. I am therefore requesting you to give me your best thinking.

If you are willing, please answer as concisely or as extensively as you desire the following questions:

What are the strengths and weaknesses of the mission program of the FMB as of now? If you want to make any comments about the CBF or the Alliance, I will welcome these too.

Given your training and experience, why have you remained with the FMB? Are you uncomfortable with the positions the SBC has taken since 1979, or does the SBC represent your position and convictions?

Would you, if given the opportunity, resign from the FMB and go to work for another mission sending agency, such as the CBF?

I recognize that these are personal questions, and you may not choose to answer them. If you do respond, I assure you that I will not divulge your names to anyone or attribute anything you say to you. If you feel you should not make any comments, I will understand. I hope, however, that you can and will respond candidly. I do want to have some input from someone I have known and respected for several years who is serving with the FMB. Feel free to say anything you like beyond the scope of the three questions. There are many other issues and things I would like to discuss with you, but I do not want you to feel you have to write a long essay.

I look forward to hearing from you.

Sincerely,

(signed) James Becker

Paul Smith's Reply

By the time Paul responded, Becker had decided that he was not going to hear from him. It was possible, he thought, that Paul did not receive the e-mail. One day in April, however, Becker turned on his computer, downloaded his e-mail, and found a message from Paul Smith. He clicked on it immediately and read the following:

Dear Dr. Becker:

We received your e-letter and were glad to hear from you. I hope you and Martha are both well and blessed in every other way too. Sorry I was not able to respond sooner. I have been traveling a lot lately, speaking in many churches, and with a WMC [World Missions Conference] starting Saturday, I will be away for another ten days. I thought I'd better respond today.

I'm sorry that I can't comment much on the CBF or the Alliance as I don't have much contact with the workings of those except that the CBF missions promoters that I've heard (Cecil Sherman and Tom Prevost) and the literature I've read always say they are different, that they are sending missionaries to unreached people groups. The impression is that pioneer missions is their only work (which is not so) and that the FMB is not doing this kind of work (even though it is). I guess I get defensive because I hear a lot of misinformation going around. I am a member of the First Baptist Church here where Tim Brown is pastor. Many of the church leaders are strong CBFers, while many members want to remain supportive of the SBC. I wouldn't want to be the pastor here. Anyway, I'm tired of it all. I'll be glad to get back to Mas Al-Mar.

(1) Weaknesses of the FMB: Fundamentalism
Strengths of the FMB: Fundamentalism

Sometimes the trustees do crazy things like defunding the seminary in Switzerland. On the other hand, the fundamental emphasis on evangelism has been helpful. The work on the field has not changed. Fortunately, our witness on the field is not affected by the SBC Executive Committee or actions by some of the seminaries' trustees.

(2) & (3) Why have I remained with the SBC?

Why not? My call has not changed. My field has not changed. Our Mission has not changed (at least, not yet). I've not been asked to do anything uncomfortable. There's work to be done and I still think the SBC is the best channel through which to do it. The support base (the churches in the US) is extensive and adequate. We still get volunteers from all types of churches, and they all do a good job. I have not been confronted with what the missionaries in Europe have confronted.

Yes, I am uncomfortable with many actions that have been taken at the SBC seminaries, etc. But I'm not going to throw out the baby with the bath water. I was irate in '91 with the Ruschlikon debacle, but a few crusading trustees are not going to make me throw my ministry away.

I must also admit to you that as the years go by, I am becoming more conservative either because of age or because of years on the mission field. I still hold to the Baptist ideals of freedom, priesthood of the believer, etc. I may not agree with some practices of the more fundamentalist pastors in the US, but I sure like their churches. As I have visited many churches this furlough, I find that the more conservative ones are becoming the most enthusiastic and supportive of missions. You've got to admit that they are the ones that are winning the lost in this country. If they can help me do the same in Mas Al-Mar, I'm all for it.

I guess you have heard about the reorganization of the FMB, and that it will soon be known as the IMB [International Board of Missions], and there will be new regions, etc. I don't know much about it yet nor how it will affect us. That remains to be seen.

Well, that's all for now. I guess I've "said my piece."

Linda went to SEBTS [Southeastern Baptist Theological Seminary] last week for Missions Week. She said it was different, but she enjoyed some aspects of it—more emphasis on spirituality and missions. She enjoyed visiting with the Braswells and others that are still around from the old days.

God bless you.

Sincerely,

(signed) Paul Smith

The Question

Becker read and re-read the letter. Paul had not said what Becker had expected, and he was troubled by what Paul did say. Was he right in stating that it would be foolish to give up his work simply because the SBC was going in a direction or doing things of which he did not approve? How should he as his former teacher respond to what Paul Smith said? Should he say anything other than thanking him for his candor?

Appendix D

Doing a Simple Mission Inventory

A. Rank the leadership and various groups in your church.

	Interest	Support	Involvement	Total
Pastor(s)	____	____	____	____
Other Staff	____	____	____	____
Lay Leaders	____	____	____	____
Men	____	____	____	____
Women	____	____	____	____
Young Adults	____	____	____	____
Adolescents	____	____	____	____
Children	____	____	____	____

5 = Continually High 4 = Periodically (Seasonally) 3 = Occasionally
2 = Infrequently/Almost Never 1 = Never

B. What mission opportunities or organizations are available for these various groups?

C. What needs to be done in mission? List some specific needs that your congregation and people could address.

Local Neighborhood:

Town or City:

Globally:

D. What are the things being done by individuals, groups, or the congregation as a whole in mission?

E. Have you taken advantage of the helps available (periodicals, speakers, studies, etc.)? If so, list some of the helps you use.

F. Are the people involved in mission being featured and heard, for example in the principal worship services?

G. What do you conclude from this inventory?

Appendix E

Kariobangi and the Disturbing Question It Raises

By Isam Ballenger, Professor of Christian Mission & World Religions, Baptist Theological Seminary at Richmond[1]

It is true that one should not weigh costs against performance when it comes to missionary work. "Performance" is an inappropriate word to use as a measure of missionary effectiveness, and costs for personnel and projects must be balanced with considerable weights of relativity. Nevertheless...

The issue could not be contained in the inactive file of my mind as our group of ten persons from the Baptist Theological Seminary stood outside the Kariobangi Baptist Youth Centre with Africa Exchange director, Sam Harrell, and the local pastor and manager, David Kiatu. Here in the midst of 785,000 very poor people is a center which offers hope to young women and men. It is no crystal cathedral, but the love and mercy of God permeate the simple building as the staff of three teaches sewing, carpentry, and the Scriptures to the young learners. If salaries cannot be paid due to insufficient income, the staff waits and hopes. Of equal importance to them are funds needed for a load of lumber to enable the youth to make furniture to sell locally. Sam brought tears to all of us when he said that if Jesus came to Nairobi, he would come first to Kariobangi. And we?

Given the size of Baptist mission work in Kenya, the question comes: why are we not involved more intimately in a work like this? Several answers come immediately. It is not a church planting work and thus does not meet our priorities. No missionary is active there and Baptists support in the main the work of missionaries. These youth do not represent an "unreached people group."

For reasons which I can explain, these answers sound hollow to me. I suppose it is because I am standing here and hearing and seeing and feeling. And I am thinking that this entire operation—building, maintenance, supplies, three salaries, scholarships for a large number of students—all this could be covered by what it costs to maintain one missionary in Kenya. How can the question be suppressed? How can we justify the answers?

[1]*Afrex* 1 (July 1998): 3. *Afrex* is a newsletter published by Africa Exchange.

Appendix F

Ten Basic Books in Mission

Anderson, Gerald Anderson, et al. *Mission Legacies: Biographical Studies of Leaders of the Modern Missionary Movement.* Maryknoll, NY: Orbis Books, 1994.

A collection of more than seventy superbly researched and written biographies of missionary leaders—Protestant, Catholic and Orthodox—from the time of William Carey to the present.

Armstrong, Karen. *A History of God.* New York: Ballentine Books, 1993.

A brilliantly written study of the origins of Judaism, Christianity, and Islam, theircommon roots and their history. Should be studied by any person genuinely interested in understanding the basic beliefs and differences in these three monotheistic faith-traditions.

Hall, Douglas John. *The End of Christendom and the Future of Christianity* Valley Forge, PA: Trinity Press, 1997.

A clear, insightful, and challenging analysis of the church and the Christian mission today. Brief—only 66 pages—but weighty. Not a lament but an affirmation of hope.

Kilbourne, Phyllis (ed.). *Street Children: A Guide to Effective Ministry.* Monrovia, CA: MARC, 1997.

Few if any studies will do more to awaken concerned church persons to the acute need for ministry to street children. Not only do the writers discuss the reasons why so many millions of children are living on the street, they offer tested methods for addressing the problem at the parish level.

Kimball, Charles. *Striving Together: A Way Forward in Christian-Muslim Relations.* Maryknoll, NY: Orbis, 1991.

A brief and engaging analysis of the history of Christian-Muslim relations, and what Christians today can do to foster understanding and reduce tensions. Exceedingly helpful for those who are serious about relating to Muslims.

Magida, Arthur J.,ed. *How to Be a Perfect Stranger.* Woodstock, VT: Jewish Lights Publishers, 1996.

The subtitle reveals the content of this unique and useful book—"A Guide to Etiquette in Other Peoples' Religious Ceremonies." Besides summarizing the history and distinctive beliefs of twenty religious traditions—including Hindu, Jewish, Buddhist, and Muslim—the chapters describe the principal features of their basic services, holy days and festivals, and life-cycle ceremonies (birth, initiation, weddings, and funerals). Appropriate attire, the question of gifts, and other issues related to each of the faiths are also addressed. A second volume is now available which includes other religions and Christian denominations.

Neely, Alan. *Christian Mission: A Case Study Approach.* Maryknoll, NY: Orbis Books, 1994.

A collection of 17 authentic case studies. Valuable for seeing and understanding the perplexing questions and dilemmas encountered by missionaries. Discussing these oft-experienced quandaries will raise the awareness of the discussants to the difficulties involved in doing mission today.

Tucker, Ruth A. *From Jerusalem to Irian Jaya.* Grand Rapids, MI: Zondervan, 1983.

A biographical history of Christian missions from the New Testament era to the present. Though written in a popular style and appealing to laypersons, this is not a breezy, superficial work. The author is probing and remarkably candid. More than one hundred thousand copies have been sold.

Robert, Dana. *American Women in Mission, 1792-1992.* Macon, GA: Mercer University Press, 1995.

A highly readable and unique study of the role of U.S. women—Protestant, Evangelical, Pentecostal, and Roman Catholic—in modern missions.

Yamamori, Tetsunao, Bryant Myers and Kenneth L. Luscombe (eds.). *Serving with the Urban Poor.* Monrovia, CA: MARC, 1998.

An analysis of the plight of the poor in the world and specifically what Christians and churches can do in mission and ministry to address this growing problem.

WORKS CITED

In the Proems

Barth, Karl. *Church Dogmatics* IV/1 (Edinburgh: T. & T. Clark, 1956) 725.

Bosch, David J. *Transforming Mission: Paradigm Shifts in Theology of Mission* (Maryknoll, NY: Orbis Books, 1991) 370, 393, 510.

Devanandan, Paul. *Christian Concern in Hinduism* (Bangalore, India: Christian Institute for the Study of Religion and Society, 1961) 116-117.

Gannaway, *Mission: Commitment to God's Hopeful Vision* (Louisville, KY: Global Mission Ministry Unit, Presbyterian Church USA, 1992) 29.

Hiebert, Paul G. *Missiological Implications of Epistemological Shifts* (Harrisburg, PA: Trinity Press, 1999) 106.

Jones, E. Stanley. *The Christ of Every Road* (New York: Abingdon, 1930) 67.

Machado, Daisy L. "Latino Church History: A Haunting Memory." *Perspectives: Hispanic Theological Initiative Occasional Papers Series 1* (Fall 1988) 27.

McKaughan, Paul, Dellanna O'Brien, and William O'Brien. *Choosing a Future for U.S. Missions* (Monrovia, CA: MARC [Missions Advanced Research Center], 1998).

O'Connor, Elizabeth. *Call to Commitment* (New York: Harper, 1963) 33.

Power, John. *Mission Theology Today* (Dublin, Ireland: Gill & McMillan, 1970) 41, 42.

Song, C. S. "Whither Protestantism in Asia Today?" *South East Asia Journal of Theology* (Spring 1970) 69.

In the Chapters

Ballenger, Isam. "Kariobangi and the Disturbing Question It Raises." *Afrex* 1 (July 1998) 3.

Black, Andrew, "Generation X Views Missions as Hands-on Proposition." *The Biblical Recorder* 165 (Jan 16, 1999) 5.

Brown, G. Thompson. *Earthen Vessels & Transcendent Power* (Maryknoll, NY: Orbis Books, 1997).

Brunner, H. Emil. *The Word in the World* (London: SCM Press, 1931).

Greenway, Roger. *Together Again* (Monrovia, CA: MARC, 1998).

Harnack, Adolf. *The Mission and Expansion of Christianity in the First Three Centuries.* Trans. James Moffatt (New York: G. P. Putnams, 1908).

Kane, J. H. "J. Hudson Taylor" in *Mission Legacies.* Ed. Gerald H. Anderson, et. al. (Mayknoll, NY: Orbis Books, 1994) 202.

Moltman, Jürgen. *The Church in the Power of the Spirit.* Trans. Margaret Kohl (New York: Harper and Row, 1977).

Nelson, Shirley. *Fair, Clear, and Terrible. The Story of Shiloh, Maine* (Latham, NY: British American Publishing, 1989.

Neill, Stephen. *A History of Christian Missions* (New York: Penguin Books, 1986).

Pierson, Paul. E. "Local Churches in Mission: What's Behind the Impatience with Traditional Mission Agencies." *International Bulletin of Missionary Research* 22 (Oct 1998): 146-150.

Roberts, W. Dayton and John A. Siewert, *Mission Handbook* (Monrovia: CA: MARC, 1989).

Verkuyl, Johannes. *Contemporary Missiology.* Trans. Dale Cooper (Grand Rapids: Eerdmans, 1978).